Something in the Basement and Other Plays

by Don Nigro

SAMUEL FRENCH, INC.
45 WEST 25TH STREET   NEW YORK 10010
7623 SUNSET BOULEVARD   HOLLYWOOD 90046
LONDON   *TORONTO*

Copyright ©, 1989, by Don Nigro

ALL RIGHTS RESERVED

CAUTION: Professionals and amateurs are hereby warned that the plays contained in this volume are subject to a royalty. They are fully protected under the copyright laws of the United States of America, the British Commonwealth, including Canada, and all other countries of the Copyright Union. All rights, including professional, amateur, motion pictures, recitation, lecturing, public reading, radio broadcasting, television, and the rights of translation into foreign languages are strictly reserved. In their present form these plays are dedicated to the reading public only.

SOMETHING IN THE BASEMENT, SCARECROW and BIBLE may be given stage presentation by amateurs in theatres seating less than 500 upon payment of a royalty of Twenty-five Dollars for the first performance, and Twenty Dollars for each additional performance **per play**. *LURKER and THE DEVIL may be given stage presentation by amateurs in theatres seating less than 500 upon payment of a royalty of Twenty Dollars for the first performance and Fifteen Dollars for each additional performance* **per play**. **Please note:** *for amateur productions in theatres seating over 500, write for special royalty quotation, giving details as to ticket price, number of performances and exact number of seats in your theatre. Royalties are payable one week before the opening performance of the play, to Samuel French, Inc., at 45 West 25th Street, New York, N.Y. 10010; or at 7623 Sunset Boulevard, Hollywood, Calif. 90046; or to Samuel French (Canada), Ltd., 80 Richmond Street East, Toronto, Ontario, Canada M5C 1P1.*

Royalty of the required amount must be paid whether the play is presented for charity or gain and whether or not admission is charged.

Stock royalty quoted on application to Samuel French, Inc.

For all other rights than those stipulated above, apply to Samuel French, Inc., 45 West 25th Street, New York, N.Y. 10010.

Particular emphasis is laid on the question of amateur or professional readings, permission and terms for which must be secured in writing from Samuel French, Inc.

Copying from this book in whole or in part is strictly forbidden by law, and the right of performance is not transferable.

Whenever the play is produced the following notice must appear on all programs, printing and advertising for the play: "Produced by special arrangement with Samuel French, Inc."

Due authorship credit must be given on all programs, printing and advertising for the play.

Printed in U.S.A.
ISBN 0 573 62523 9

BILLING AND CREDIT REQUIREMENTS

All producers of SOMETHING IN THE BASEMENT AND OTHER PLAYS *must* give credit to the Author in all programs and in all instances in which the title of any Play appears for purposes of advertising, publicizing or otherwise exploiting the Play and/or production. The author's name *must* appear on a separate line in which no other name appears, immediately following the title of the play, and *must* appear in size of type not less than fifty percent the size of title type.

Anyone presenting the play shall not commit or authorize any act or omission by which the copyright of the play or the right to copyright same may be impaired.

No changes shall be made in the play for the purpose of your production unless authorized in writing.

The publication of this play does not imply that it is necessarily available for performance by amateurs or professionals. Amateurs and professionals considering a production are strongly advised in their own interests to apply to Samuel French, Inc., for consent before starting rehearsals, advertising, or booking a theatre or hall.

No part of this book may be reproduced, stored in a retrieval system, or transmitted in any form, by any means, including mechanical, electronic, photocopying, recording, or otherwise, without the prior written permission of the publisher.

SOMETHING IN THE BASEMENT

CHARACTERS:

Mary, an attractive woman in her early thirties
Philip, her husband, late thirties

SETTING:

A bedroom, a kitchen, and a door in the kitchen leading to the basement. The bed is real, the door to the basement is practical and very sturdy, and some suggestion of cabinets and sink with window above is necessary, but most of the rest of the set should only be suggested, and a detailed realistic environment, beyond what is actually used in the play itself, is not desirable.

Something in the Basement was first produced on September 28, 1979 in the Maclean Theatre at the University of Iowa in Iowa City, with the following cast:

MARY	Kate McKillup
PHILIP	David Simkins

It was directed by Sue Hickerson.

Something in the Basement

1

(Night. Ticking clock. Crickets. PHILIP and MARY in bed, both reading, one lamp over the bed. He puts down his book and stares at her for a long moment.)

MARY. *(not looking up from her book)* Don't bother, Philip.
PHILIP. Don't bother what?
MARY. Don't bother ME.
PHILIP. I wasn't bothering you.
MARY. You were about to bother me.
PHILIP. Well, why shouldn't I? You're my wife. I can bother my wife. A man can bother his wife. Isn't that written somewhere? I've often bothered you in the past. You've told me so. As a matter of fact, on occasion, you've bothered ME, from time to time. I remember.
MARY. Well, cherish your memories.
PHILIP. This doesn't mean, I hope, that you don't intend to ever allow me to bother you again. *(She continues reading.)* Mary? Why shouldn't I bother you?
MARY. *(looking over the top of her book)* Because when no creation is possible, when nothing can possibly be created, when the act leads not to any created thing, then the act itself, however pleasurable it may once have been, no matter what the intention, becomes, ultimately, ridiculous and obscene, and those who engage in the act become likewise ridiculous and obscene, and this, Philip, is the reason you shouldn't bother me. *(pause)*

PHILIP. Oh. (*She is reading. He thinks about that. Then he turns off the light. Darkness.*)

MARY. (*after a moment, still holding the book before her eyes in the dark*) I take it you've finished reading. (*Silence from him.*) I gather from your silence that you agree with me on this matter of bothering and unbothering, and that you have no further intention of bothering me, possibly ever. Am I mistaken? (*silence*) I gather from your silence that I am not mistaken. (*She closes her book.*) The sound you just heard was me closing my book. Now I am going to sleep. (*PHILIP turns on the light.*) It is customary, you know, Philip, in most civilized countries, to read in the light and sleep in the dark.

PHILIP. We can adopt something.

MARY. Good night, Philip. (*She turns the light off. They sit in the dark.*)

PHILIP. I said—

MARY. Yes, I heard what you said, I have not yet resorted to placing objects in my ears to avoid hearing what you say to me, although I do not rule out that possibility in the near future. You said 'thing.' Adopt some 'thing.' I do not wish to adopt a thing.

PHILIP. I mean a child. Infant. Baby. Tot. Offspring. Nursling. Suckling. Changeling.

MARY. I think a suckling would be nice. We could get a little pig, and I could nurse it and dress it up in a little bonnet, and take it everywhere. Then when it got older and began to grow fat and ugly, we could put an apple in its mouth and have a luau.

PHILIP. (*putting his hand on hers*) Mary—

MARY. (*pulling her hand gingerly away*) No touching, please. My cousin was adopted. She found out when she was seventeen. She went berserk. She ran amok. I would not like my little suckling to run amok.

SOMETHING IN THE BASEMENT 7

PHILIP. Our suckling would not run amok. I'd be willing to virtually guarantee this in writing. I'd stake my life on it. I feel that strongly about it.

MARY. No. Absolutely not. And in the future, keep your hands to yourself, please. You don't know about these things. You never had a cousin.

PHILIP. Your family history is not relevant here. It's OUR family history which concerns me at present. Or the possible complete future lack of family history. Or the complete possible lack of future family history. I believe you know what I'm attempting to say.

MARY. I haven't a clue.

PHILIP. I'm trying to say that I need to touch you. Sometimes I need to touch you. I don't think that's an unreasonable position for me to take. I just need, now and then—

MARY. Listen.

PHILIP. I just don't see why we can't—

MARY. Shut up and listen.

PHILIP. What?

MARY. Didn't you hear that?

PHILIP. No.

MARY. I heard something.

PHILIP. Where?

MARY. I think in the basement.

PHILIP. There's nothing in the basement.

MARY. Listen. (*They listen.*) There. Do you hear it now?

PHILIP. No.

MARY. I heard it. I DID hear it. (*Pause. He turns on the light.*)

PHILIP. All right. (*He gets out of bed.*)

MARY. Oh, don't go. You don't have to go.

PHILIP. No, I want to go. I live for opportunities like

this. I'm tremendously excited about it. (*He goes into the kitchen and begins rattling around in drawers.*) It's like an old movie. George and Gracie. Ozzie and Harriet. Dagwood and Blondie. Laurel and Hardy. I'm W.C. Fields. I go into the basement and sing harmony with the burglars. (*He sings.*)
Oh, the sycamores
are dripping on
the Wabash—

MARY. Stop that. Be quiet.

PHILIP. Are you afraid I'll scare the burglars?

MARY. I'm afraid you'll scare the neighbors. What are you doing?

PHILIP. I'm getting a flashlight. Is that all right with you? Or would you prefer I use my X-ray vision?

MARY. Why don't you just turn on the light?

PHILIP. There's no electricity in the basement.

MARY. There's a bulb at the bottom of the steps.

PHILIP. It doesn't work.

MARY. Well, replace it, then.

PHILIP. Okay, maybe I can get one of the burglars to hold the ladder for me, what do you think? How many burglars does it take to change a light bulb?

MARY. Philip, it's all right, come back to bed.

PHILIP. What, and miss an opportunity like this? Not me. I only get one chance at life, Mary. I've got to jump on my opportunities when they present themselves. (*He's found a flashlight. He opens the basement door, shines the light down into the dark.*) Hi down there. Want to come up and have some popcorn? (*Silence. He starts down the stairs.*) Peek a boooo. Hel-lo-ooooo. (*Sound of his footsteps going down. MARY waits nervously in bed. Pause.*)

SOMETHING IN THE BASEMENT

MARY. Is something down there? (*A SHARP SOUND, like a table sliding on cement.*)
PHILIP. OWWWWWWW.
MARY. Philip?
PHILIP. Shit.
MARY. Are you all right?
PHILIP. Compared to when?
MARY. What's down there?
PHILIP. Spiders. Old furniture. Bunch of junk. Dead bodies. A camel. Two armadillos. Wait a minute.
MARY. What is it? What do you see? (*No answer.*) Phil? (*A FAINT NOISE, like tinkling glass.*) Philip? (*The sound of his footsteps coming up the steps. He appears in the kitchen, closes the basement door, puts the flashlight away, goes back and latches the door, then goes into the bedroom. He is carrying a green bottle with a round bottom.*) Well?
PHILIP. The camel says hello.
MARY. What's that?
PHILIP. It's a green bottle.
MARY. What's it for?
PHILIP. I don't know. The bottom's round. It won't stand up.
MARY. Did you see anything?
PHILIP. Nobody home. Why would anybody want to make a bottle that won't stand up?
MARY. I heard something.
PHILIP. There's nobody down there. You want to go down and have a look for yourself, be my guest. (*He puts the bottle down and gets into bed.*)
MARY. I don't like basements.
PHILIP. Fine, then let's go to sleep. (*He turns off the light. Pause.*)

MARY. What's it like down there?

PHILIP. You've seen what it's like.

MARY. Only from the top of the steps. In the daytime. I never open that door at night. Tell me what it's like.

PHILIP. It's dark.

MARY. I know it's dark.

PHILIP. It's old. Like the house. Corridors and rooms. Little wooden doors that lead to other rooms. People had big cellars in the old days.

MARY. Why?

PHILIP. I don't know. Cans. Canning. Tomatoes. Potatoes. Rhubarb. Wine. Runaway slaves. All manner of things.

MARY. Maybe it's an embalming bottle.

PHILIP. (*starting to doze off*) Pardon?

MARY. They hang upside down. Like bats. The embalming fluid oozes down into the body. And one is—more or less—preserved.

PHILIP. That's charming.

MARY. You didn't go into all the rooms. Did you? I mean, you didn't open every door. You didn't examine every possible hiding place. You weren't down there long enough for that. Something could be down there. Somebody. Did you latch the door? Philip? Did you latch the door when you came back up? (*Pause. The ticking clock in the dark.*) I'm cold. (*pause*) Philip? Are you asleep? (*pause*) Make love to me. I want you to make love to me. Philip? (*pause*) Philip?

2

(*Bird sounds. Morning. PHILIP and MARY are dressing.*)

SOMETHING IN THE BASEMENT

PHILIP. Nice morning.
MARY. Is it?
PHILIP. Did you sleep all right?
MARY. I had bad dreams.
PHILIP. About basements?
MARY. I don't think you searched it thoroughly enough. You finished too soon.
PHILIP. I finished when I was done.
MARY. You were done too soon.
PHILIP. I've been thinking.
MARY. Don't strain yourself.
PHILIP. Your father died in the basement.
MARY. Who told you that?
PHILIP. Your mother.
MARY. My mother is an idiot.
PHILIP. I know, but it's true, though, isn't it? Your mother's idiocy notwithstanding. Your father died in the basement.
MARY. Not this basement. Some other basement.
PHILIP. And now you're terrified of basements.
MARY. This man has a great future in popular psychology.
PHILIP. When you have an unreasonable, though perfectly understandable, fear like that, the best thing you can do is to recognize it, meet it head on.
MARY. This man should write self-help books. He could make a fortune writing advice columns in the newspapers. This man is an oracle.
PHILIP. You know I'm right.
MARY. Dear Doctor Phil — My husband and I are unable to make babies together. What should I do? Get a cat? Find charity work? Raise chinchillas?
PHILIP. Mary, if you want children —
MARY. Maybe I could start collecting embalming bot-

tles. That'd be a nice, harmless hobby for the little woman. What do you think, Doc?

PHILIP. I'm trying to help you, but you won't let me.

MARY. People who love each other don't want to help each other.

PHILIP. Of course they do.

MARY. No they don't.

PHILIP. Yes they do.

MARY. You have no brain, Philip. Your mouth works, but it's not connected to anything. Words come out, you appear to be constructing meaningful sentences, but in reality, it's all an illusion, like sawing a woman in half. (*He looks at her. Then he goes into the kitchen.*) Oh, don't go away mad. Do you know that you smelled there for a minute like Orchard Hill? Isn't that odd? I used to ride bareback on Orchard Hill, and the smell of rotting apples in the autumn was overpowering, and one day I met a young man on the path, and I stopped to talk to him, I knew him slightly, and it was October, and I got off the horse and tied it to a tree by a pile of rotting apples, and the young man and I took a walk through the leaves behind the farmhouse by the creek, and we sat in the leaves and kissed, and he touched my breasts, I allowed him to touch my breasts, I don't know why, exactly, I think it was the smell of autumn and the rotting apples, and the bareback riding had perhaps something to do with it, in any case, one thing led to another, and before long, as if we'd come there for exactly that purpose he was making love to me in the leaves, I remember wondering as he was pulling off my underpants if there might be small children watching, I know the horse was watching, he was a gelding, I believe, but it was so nice to feel bare flesh against one in the cool October twilight that I decided I didn't care, as I could feel welling up in me the most incredible orgasm, staring up at the sky as he pressed me with each thrust deeper into the leaves, and when he shuddered I felt it squirting deep inside me, and then everything was still and the air was full of the smell of rotting apples. Odd that you, of all people, should suddenly, one morning, apropos of nothing, begin to smell like that. On the other hand, perhaps it isn't you at all. Perhaps the smell has come wafting up through the registers from the basement. Do you think that's it? Philip? (*He goes out. MARY is alone.*)

3

(*MARY peeling apples in the kitchen. PHILIP comes in from outside.*)

PHILIP. Come outside a minute.
MARY. I don't want to come outside. It's cold outside.
PHILIP. No it's not. I want to show you something.
MARY. Describe it.
PHILIP. I don't want to describe it, I want you to see it.
MARY. But I trust you, Philip. Your descriptive powers are more than adequate on most occasions, I believe. Your problem is not description. Your problem is life.
PHILIP. It's cats.
MARY. Your problem is cats?
PHILIP. Come out and look.
MARY. You want me to come out and look at cats?
PHILIP. In the basement. You heard cats. There's a broken window around back.
MARY. Did you see any cats?
PHILIP. I smelled cats. I saw one in the yard.

MARY. But did you actually SEE any particular cat going into or out of our basement window?

PHILIP. I didn't have to see it.

MARY. Did you go into the basement and observe at first hand cats nesting there, making homes, having intercourse, raising little families in among the canned rhubarb and the embalming bottles?

PHILIP. I really think that's the best explanation.

MARY. Did you go back into the basement and look?

PHILIP. Briefly.

MARY. You accept a great deal on faith, Philip, you know that?

PHILIP. I saw the broken window. I smelled cats. There was a cat in the yard. You heard noises at night. Cats move about at night. There are dozens of cats in this neighborhood. There are cats in the garden. There are cats on the porch. There are cats on the roof. Generations of kittens are born in the tool shed. It makes perfectly good sense.

MARY. But you don't know, you don't know, this is circumstantial evidence, it might have been any kind of animal, a racoon, an opossum, a groundhog, a squirrel, a chipmunk, a rat, a family of marmosets. Mightn't it have been marmoset musk you smelled? Are you some sort of olfactory whiz in the area of small furry animals? Did you study this in college?

PHILIP. Do you have a better suggestion?

MARY. Yes, I think we should move out.

PHILIP. We just moved in.

MARY. Well, that's life, Philip, in and out, in and out.

PHILIP. Why do you want to move?

MARY. I don't know, it's just the gypsy in my soul. Don't you have any gypsy in your soul? Probably you've got embalming fluid.

PHILIP. You're the one that wanted to move here.

MARY. I'm allowed to change my mind. It's written into the marriage contract.

PHILIP. Why aren't you happy here?

MARY. I didn't say I wasn't happy here. I'm ecstatic. I'm orgasmic, in my own quiet way.

PHILIP. Why the hell can't you just talk to me for once like a normal human being?

MARY. Because I'm not a normal human being, Philip, I'm from the planet Vulva, and I've come here to abduct your sexual organs, if I can find them.

PHILIP. Do you know what you are?

MARY. I wouldn't get too close to a woman's knife, Philip, when she's peeling apples. Didn't they teach you that in college? (*pause*) No. What am I?

PHILIP. I'm boarding it up. I've found some boards and I'm boarding up the broken window nice and tight. I've been all around the house, and that's the only opening I can find. I promise you, nothing is ever going to get into our basement again.

MARY. The question now is, will anything ever get out? (*He looks at her. She peels apples.*)

4

(*The bedroom, night. PHILIP and MARY are undressing.*)

MARY. Put out the light.
PHILIP. Why?
MARY. Put it out.
PHILIP. I'm undressing.
MARY. You don't need a light for that.

PHILIP. I want to read.

MARY. While you're undressing?

PHILIP. I thought maybe after. Is that all right?

MARY. You can turn it on and off, you know. It's a wonderful invention, it really is. Let me show you how it works. (*She marches over and turns the light off. He turns it back on.*)

PHILIP. What's the matter with you?

MARY. I just want the light off. Is that too much to ask? I'm not asking you to kiss my foot or lick the newspaper in the birdcage, I just want the light off, is that going to damage you emotionally or something?

PHILIP. Mary, I think we should talk.

MARY. All right, why don't you start without me, I'll be in the bathroom. (*She goes into the bathroom.*)

PHILIP. Mary? What are you doing in the bathroom?

MARY. Is that really any of your business? Do I ask you what you're doing in here at any given moment? Are you keeping records?

PHILIP. Are you undressing in the bathroom?

MARY. What if I am? Is it a violation of international law?

PHILIP. Why don't you undress out here?

MARY. I don't want you watching me.

PHILIP. Why not? Mary, why not?

MARY. I don't know.

PHILIP. I've seen you, Mary.

MARY. Then why do you care?

PHILIP. I've seen you naked thousands of times. I've examined minutely every part of your body. I've touched every part of your body with every part of my body. Why can't you undress in front of me? Why can't you put your nightgown on in front of your husband, Mary? Is it leprosy? Have you got warts? Body warts?

SOMETHING IN THE BASEMENT

Carbuncles? Elephantiasis? Are you growing a third breast?

MARY. (*emerging in nightgown*) It's not really that I don't want you to see me naked.

PHILIP. Well, what is it, then?

MARY. It's that I don't want to see YOU naked. (*She turns out the light and gets into bed.*)

PHILIP. Why not? Why the hell not?

MARY. Go to sleep, Philip.

PHILIP. I've got feelings, too, you know. You're not the only one with feelings here.

MARY. Do we care?

PHILIP. I don't know. Do we? (*No answer. He gets into bed.*)

MARY. Stay on your side of the bed.

PHILIP. I'm on my side.

MARY. Stay more on your side.

PHILIP. If I was any further on my side I'd be in the kitchen.

MARY. That's fine with me.

PHILIP. We've got to talk about this, and we've got to talk about it now.

MARY. I'm tired. I'm going to sleep. I'm sleeping now.

PHILIP. Mary?

MARY. I'm sleeping.

PHILIP. I don't know what I'd do without you. Probably I'd go crazy. I think I'd go crazy.

MARY. Don't do that.

PHILIP. Don't go crazy?

MARY. Don't press your erect member against my buttocks.

PHILIP. I thought you were sleeping.

MARY. A woman can feel that in her sleep, trust me.

PHILIP. But you're talking.

MARY. I'm talking in my sleep. I also bite in my sleep, so get your hand off my breast.

PHILIP. I've been thinking.

MARY. You can think with your hand someplace else.

PHILIP. All right.

MARY. Not there.

PHILIP. How about here?

MARY. Do you know what your problem is, Philip? Your problem is that I don't like you. (*pause*) I believe he's actually retreated. I am unable to detect the pressure of any of his sharp appendages upon my person. Can it be that my husband has suddenly died? (*pause*) I liked you once. I liked you very much. You were very mysterious. Capable. This excited me. There were things about you I didn't understand, felt I could perhaps never properly understand. I liked you then. To be honest, Philip, I couldn't keep my hands off you then. I would ambush you in hallways. Seduce you in other people's houses. Put my hand in your pants while you drove at night. I was horribly jealous and possessive, then, I know. You were very strange and wonderful and I refused to share you with anybody or anything. And I didn't. (*pause*) You don't have any friends, do you, Philip? You used to have friends, I seem to recall. Not many, not nearly as many as me, of course, but you did have friends. I guess I put a stop to that, didn't I? I didn't like any of your friends, so I made you choose. And you always chose me. Every time. Always. (*pause*) That was really boring of you, Philip. (*pause*) You were never unfaithful to me, either, were you? I can't imagine you being unfaithful to me. Once I could imagine it. And imagination whetted jealousy. It was all rather erotic. But you never did. (*pause*) I myself —(*pause*) I myself want to have lots of friends. (*Pause. A SOUND like wind chimes and a kind of shuffling.*) Philip? PHILIP.

SOMETHING IN THE BASEMENT

PHILIP. Hmmmmmmmmm?

MARY. Philip, did you hear that?

PHILIP. Good night, Gracie.

MARY. There's something down there. I heard it very clearly.

PHILIP. Great. I walled up a cat. I have walled the monster up within the tomb.

MARY. It isn't a cat. I know it isn't. It's something else.

PHILIP. If it isn't a cat, then what is it?

MARY. I don't know. That's what you're supposed to go down and find out.

PHILIP. I am NOT going back down there.

MARY. But there's something in the basement.

PHILIP. Well, it can just stay there because I don't care.

MARY. You're afraid. That's what it is. You're afraid to go down into the basement. (*Pause. He turns on the light.*)

PHILIP. I just want it recorded for posterity that I don't like this. I don't like getting up in the middle of the night with some woman I used to know screaming at me about imaginary things crawling in the basement. This is not, I think, conducive to good mental health. I do not want to get out of my nice warm bed where my wife who used to be nice and warm used to keep me nice and warm, where I am no longer very nice and warm but where the hope that some day perhaps in the future before I die of acute marital tension I will once again be nice and warm, I do not wish to leave this womblike place where at least the memory of warmth and the possibility of warmth still exist, for where there is memory there is at least possibility, and one lives on that, on possibility, one's ethic is an ethic of possibility, one clings to strands of possibility, that warmth remembered is at least a fragment of hope that warmth is possible again. I do not want to give this up, and yet I go, down into the bowels of the ancient house and deep into the filthy, musty, cobweb-ridden labyrinthine basement, to rescue an imaginary cat. Notice that I go. As a testament to my desperation and the memory of your lovely naked flesh shivering under my fingertips.

MARY. Now you hate me.

PHILIP. Nonsense. I'm much too boring to hate you. Didn't they teach you that in college? (*He goes into the kitchen, gets the flashlight, opens the basement door, looks down, and goes down the steps. MARY gets out of bed, goes into the kitchen, looks down the steps. From below, the faint SOUND of tinkling glass, and a shuffling noise.*)

MARY. Philip? You can come up if you want. I don't mean to make you go down there if you don't want to. Philip? (*A loud crash.*) Philip? (*Footsteps up the stairs. MARY moves back to the bedroom door, frightened. PHILIP appears.*)

PHILIP. Hi there.

MARY. Are you all right?

PHILIP. (*closing the door behind him*) Of course I'm all right. Why shouldn't I be?

MARY. What was that noise?

PHILIP. Noise?

MARY. I heard noises. And a crash.

PHILIP. (*putting the flashlight back in the drawer*) Something fell over.

MARY. What fell over?

PHILIP. I think it was me.

MARY. Why didn't you answer me?

PHILIP. I didn't want to bore you. (*He goes back into the bedroom. She follows.*)

MARY. So, did you find out what it was?

PHILIP. I didn't see anything.

SOMETHING IN THE BASEMENT

MARY. You searched the whole basement?

PHILIP. I looked, I looked, all right?

MARY. You found something and you just don't want to tell me. You think I'll be frightened. What is it, Philip? Tell me. You're holding out on me, I know you are.

PHILIP. You're right, Mary. I'm lying. Actually, there's a man in a mask down there, playing an organ.

MARY. I heard something. I did. I heard it.

PHILIP. I'm tired, and I've got to go to work in the morning. If you don't like me any more, okay. If you don't want me to see you without your clothes on, if you don't want to see me without my clothes on, okay. If you don't want me to touch you, if you don't want to make love, if you don't want to have children, if you don't want to talk about it, all right, fine, great, excuse me for intruding upon your life, but at least let me get some sleep, do you mind? And if you're so damn interested in what's in the basement, then why the hell don't you just go down there and have a look for yourself, what do you say, kid?

MARY. That's not fair.

PHILIP. I think it's fair. I think it's a wonderful idea. Go on down and see for yourself. (*MARY looks at him.*) Don't care to? Fine. Then just shut up and let me get some sleep. Even the boring require sleep now and then. (*He gets into bed. MARY looks at him. Then she turns and goes back into the kitchen. She opens the basement door and looks down the steps.*)

MARY. It smells good down there. You can smell it up through the registers in the daytime, it moves through the whole house, sometimes, a kind of musty salamander smell, old houses, earth, my father's house, old things. Rotting apples. (*She looks down the steps.*) You talk to me that way because you're sure I wouldn't dare.

PHILIP. Just come to bed. I won't bother you.

MARY. You hide your own cowardice by accusing me.

PHILIP. I don't know what you want.

MARY. My fear comforts you. It does. (*She looks down into the basement. Then she gets the flashlight, hesitates at the top, and goes down the steps.*)

PHILIP. Mary? What are you doing in there? Mary? (*pause*) I miss you. (*pause*) Mary?

5

(*Morning. Bird sounds. PHILIP sits on the edge of the bed. Sound of the shower from off.*)

PHILIP. I didn't hear you come back to bed last night.

MARY. (*from off, in the shower*) What?

PHILIP. I didn't hear you come back.

MARY. You were asleep.

PHILIP. Not for a long time.

MARY. But you WERE asleep. (*She has turned off the water.*)

PHILIP. Did you find anything interesting in the basement?

MARY. It's rather nice down there, actually.

PHILIP. Is it?

MARY. Yes. You were right, about confronting one's fears, and all that. It was very stimulating.

PHILIP. Stimulating?

MARY. (*entering, in bathrobe*) Why didn't you come down and join me?

PHILIP. I didn't want to spoil it for you.

MARY. (*brushing her hair*) I don't see how you could have. (*She brushes. He watches her. He goes over and puts his arms around her from behind, kissing her neck, fumbling at her robe.*) What are you doing?

PHILIP. I want to make love to you.

MARY. Now?

PHILIP. Yes, now.

MARY. In the morning?

PHILIP. It's been known to happen in the morning. I've heard stories, anyway. (*He is caressing and kissing her, moving her towards the bed.*) Come on.

MARY. You'll be late for work.

PHILIP. I don't care.

MARY. I've just taken a shower.

PHILIP. (*getting her onto the bed*) Take another one.

MARY. Are you afraid of the dark, Philip?

PHILIP. (*getting her robe undone*) You look wonderful this morning. You smell so good. Your body is so soft and warm, you feel so good —

MARY. There's nothing to be ashamed of, if you are. Lots of men are afraid of things. It's nothing you should lose any sleep over. I mean, don't let it take the lead out of your pencil. (*He stops, poised above her.*)

PHILIP. I don't like that expression. It's vulgar.

MARY. So is rape. (*Pause. PHILIP looks at her. Then he gets up, goes over and leans against the doorframe. She sits up.*) I don't think any less of you for being afraid. Women have almost as many fears as men do, you know.

PHILIP. I'm not afraid of anything.

MARY. Well, that's an extraordinary position to take.

PHILIP. What were you doing down there all that time?

MARY. What were YOU doing up HERE all that time?

PHILIP. I was waiting for you.

MARY. That's good, Philip. They also serve who only

stand and wait. (*She goes back into the bathroom. PHILIP goes over to the bed, picks up a pillow, and holds it.*)

6

(*Night. MARY and PHILIP in bed in the dark.*)

MARY. Do you know what I did today? I started painting again. It's the most extraordinary thing. I haven't done a thing in over a year, and then suddenly, today, I just couldn't wait, I painted most of the day, isn't that odd?

PHILIP. What are you painting?

MARY. It's a picture of a woman lying on her back, on a kind of old sofa, in a dark place, with cobwebs, quite naked, and there is this figure above her, rather obscured by the cobwebs and shadows, this figure about to thrust into her, it's as if, I don't know, she has this look on her face, this sort of ecstasy, the figure has these big, rough hands and one is caressing her right breast, the thumb pressing across her erect nipple, and the other hand is under the small of her back, so that she's partially lifted up, with her legs hanging down, and her arms behind her head, holding onto the sofa, and her hair streaming down, her body arched, just about to be thrust into, and the look on her face, that's the difficult thing to capture, the look on her face is — Philip, don't. Philip, please. Stop it. Not tonight, all right?

PHILIP. If you'd just relax and —

MARY. I said stop it.

PHILIP. Mary, sex is not just something one paints in

pictures. Surveys have shown that nine out of ten young married couples have sex at least once a year. There is nothing wrong with sex.

MARY. Everything is wrong with sex, that's what makes it so exciting, but not tonight. Stop it. Listen. There it is again. Listen. (*She turns on the light.*) You must have heard it that time.

PHILIP. (*beating his head quietly against the headboard, clunk, clunk, clunk*) I didn't hear anything. I don't want to hear anything. I just want my wife back. (*She gets up and goes into the kitchen.*) Mary. (*She is getting the flashlight.*) Now listen to me.

MARY. It's all right. There's not a thing to worry about. You just go back to sleep. You've got to get up and go to work in the morning. (*She opens the basement door and starts down.*)

PHILIP. Don't go down there.

MARY. You're quite welcome to come along. That might be fun. (*Her footsteps going down. He comes into the kitchen and hesitates at the stairs.*)

PHILIP. I'm not playing games. I refuse to play games. I'm not good at games. Mary? (*He paces back and forth, increasingly upset.*) This is rapidly getting out of control here. There was a time when I preferred to humor you. In everything. In every single matter. But I think that time has passed. I think that was a grave miscalculation in strategy on my part. In fact, it seems to me — (*a small, delighted laugh from MARY below*) Are you all right? (*She laughs again.*) What's going on down there? (*The SOUND of the tinkling glass. MARY's laughter. The shuffling noise.*) Mary?

MARY. Philip, come down here.

PHILIP. I don't want to come down there.

MARY. You don't know what you're missing.

PHILIP. I don't want to know what I'm missing. I don't care what I'm missing.

MARY. Philip, it's not at all what you think. Not at all. Come down and see.

PHILIP. I don't think you understand me. I don't think you understand just who you're dealing with here.

MARY. I need you, Philip. I need you to come down here.

PHILIP. And after a while I think it becomes a matter of principle, and of taste, and of human freedom. I think it becomes a matter of personal dignity and self respect. (*He is growing more nervous and upset.*) I'd love to come down to the basement. God knows, it might be the highlight of my adult life, to feel my bare feet on the cold slime, to hear the water dripping again, feel little furry things creeping across my feet in the dark. (*The TINKLING NOISE. Shuffling. Laughter from MARY.*) I know you've been upset. (*She laughs more, not so much at PHILIP but as if conspiring with someone.*) I've been upset. I've tried everything to please you. And all I've succeeded in doing—

MARY. (*a laugh that turns into little sounds of sexual pleasure*) Ohhhh. Oooooooooooo. Ohhhhhh.

PHILIP. —all I've succeeded in doing is driving you into this other place, this place you hide in, a place I apparently can never—

MARY. OHHHHHHHH. Oh, God. Oh. OHHHHHHHHH.

PHILIP. And this leads me to believe that civilized man—

MARY. Uh. Uh. Uh. Uh. Uh. Uh.

PHILIP. That man in civilization has perhaps—

MARY. Oh. OHHH. Ohhhhhhh.

PHILIP. —that perhaps somewhere along the line—
MARY. OHHHH. OHHHHHH. OHHHHHHHH. JESUS.
PHILIP. —that somewhere along the way—
MARY. OHHHH. OHHHHH. GOD. OH, GODD.
PHILIP. —a terrible mistake has been made.
MARY. YES. GOD. YES. OHHHH. UHHHHH. UHHHHHHHHHHH.
PHILIP. A tragic mistake.
MARY. OHHHHHHHH. OHHHHHHHHHH.
PHILIP. And I think—
MARY. UHHHHHH. UHHHHHH. UHHHHHHHHHHH.
PHILIP. I believe—
MARY. UHHHHHHHH. AAAHHHHHHH. AAAHHHHHH. UHHHHHHHH. (*PHILIP goes into the bedroom and stands by the bed as MARY's cries build to a climax. He turns off the light and stands there in the dark.*) UHHHHHHHHHHHHH. UHHHHHHHHHHHH. UHHHHHHHHHHHHH. UHHHHHHHHHHHH. Uhhhhhhhhhhhhhhhhhhhhhhhhhhhhhhhhh.

(*silence*)

7

(*Day. PHILIP sits in his pyjamas in the kitchen. MARY comes in from outside with a bag of groceries.*)

MARY. Are you still sitting there? What's the matter with you? Are you sick? Philip? Did you call in to work? Hello? Should I get a doctor? Notify next of kin? You're pouting. You're upset that I went down into the basement last night. Don't pout. There's no reason to pout. I mean, it's OUR basement. It's not like I was going down into some strange man's basement or anything like that, is it? Do you want some soup? I can make you some nice oyster soup if you want. How about a cup of tea? We have ginseng. Would you like a massage? You're thinking, aren't you? It's good that you're thinking. I like a man who thinks. Well, sometimes. Not all the time. I do hope you're thinking about ME. Are you thinking about me? (*No answer.*) You know, Philip, if I thought there was some part of you, something, any part of you I hadn't seen already, that would excite me tremendously. I like a man of mystery. That excites me. I get all excited. If I thought you were capable of anything I hadn't seen before, could not have predicted, I would become horribly, uncontrollably excited. Do you understand that? Do you see what I mean? (*No answer.*) You have, in reality, as a matter of fact, plenty of lead in your pencil. You have, actually, rather too MUCH lead in your pencil. I don't believe I've ever in my life known a man with so much lead in his pencil. You have enough lead for two pencils, for an entire pencil box. And you're very good. I mean, you're quite a good lover, in reality, very attentive, and tender. And passionate. Oh, yes, once we get going, Philip, I'm quite happy with you. I really am. It's just that lately the whole business of GETTING going has just seemed not worth it. There is no child. There will be no child. And there is no mystery in the getting, no danger in it. Do you see that? Philip? Do you think perhaps you could surprise me, somehow? Do something unexpected? I like this silence. It's different, at least. It's a beginning. I guess. Of what, I don't know. And I rather like not knowing. Except that I also want desperately to know. Well, maybe not desperately. What are you thinking about? Philip? (*He goes into the bedroom, gets into bed, lays there.*) What are you thinking?

8

(*Night. PHILIP in bed, light on, not reading, looking at his hands. MARY is undressing.*)

MARY. Still at it, are we? I wish you'd tell me. Look, I'm undressing, right here in your presence tonight, and with the light on. What do you think about THAT, Philip? Do you feel honored? Do you remember breasts? Do you remember my thighs and my stomach? You remember sex, don't you, Philip? You remember kissing and hugging, caressing, rubbing, all manner of foreplay. You remember oral sex. You recall the moment of mounting, the moment of penetration, the sliding in, the tangle of flesh and sweat and hair, the bizarre noises, the sound of the bed, the ecstasy of the animals, the manic clutching and the altered reality. Passion alters reality. That's why it's so nice. If you wanted to, you know, it's entirely possible that, with the right kind of persuasion, you might be able to seduce me tonight. It's not certain, of course, but it's possible. Would you like to seduce me?

PHILIP. I've been having a dream, the last two nights. I go through the door, walk down the steps into the basement, darkness before me, and looking back, at the top of the steps, where I've just been, I see a small rectangle of light, I walk to the foot of the steps and I stand there, trembling, I feel the cold inside my pyjamas. It smells of old earth, corridor and labyrinth, rotten apples. Before me is darkness and your laughter, very faint. I hesitate. There is a small gust of wind, very slight, like the house sighing, and the door at the top of the steps swings shut, and I am lost, in total darkness. (*pause*)

MARY. What I dream about is our child. Our child is like my father, very pale and cold. A pale, cold child, playing an organ. A spider walks on his lips. From down in the basement I can look up and see a small rectangle of light at the top of the steps, and I know that's you. And this comforts me. There is great comfort in that, for some reason. Make love to me now. I need you now. Make love to me. (*She leans down to kiss him, presses herself against him, on top of him, kissing him, and then—*)

PHILIP. Did you hear that?

MARY. What?

PHILIP. I heard something.

MARY. No, I don't think so.

PHILIP. Yes, clearly, I heard it, very clearly, something in the basement.

MARY. Is there?

PHILIP. Oh yes, yes, I'm certain.

MARY. I don't care, Philip, I want you to make love to me.

PHILIP. But I heard it.

MARY. Philip—

PHILIP. I tell you, I heard it, I did.

MARY. Forget about that right now.

PHILIP. But it's a great occasion, Mary. On this particular night I have heard, actually heard, definitely, without any question, undeniably heard something in the basement.

MARY. Well, congratulations, Philip; now that we've got that all taken care of—

PHILIP. But shouldn't this be investigated?

MARY. Oh, don't bother with that now, please—

SOMETHING IN THE BASEMENT

PHILIP. No, not me. You.

MARY. Me?

PHILIP. Yes. You.

MARY. I don't want to go down in the basement, Philip, I want you to make love to me.

PHILIP. I really think you need to investigate this matter right away, Mary. I really feel very strongly about this.

MARY. You heard it, you go.

PHILIP. No, but you're the brave one, you're the expert, you're the one who longs for mystery and adventure, you're the one who's bored to death with ordinary life, you're the one who seems to have such a good time down there, I think you should be the one.

MARY. I'd really very, very much rather just—

PHILIP. Mary, if you don't go down and see what's in the basement, right now, immediately, so I can have some peace of mind, do you know what I'm going to do? I'm going to board up the door, and that way, nobody will ever be able to go down into our basement again.

MARY. What about the gas man?

PHILIP. Not the gas man, not the electric man, not the boogey man, not you, not me, nobody.

MARY. Oh, come on, Philip, you wouldn't do that.

PHILIP. I have the tools. I have the boards and the nails. I have a hammer. I brought them in from the garage while you were out buying groceries. They're in the cupboard under the sink. Go and look if you like. I've planned it very carefully. I think I'll go do it right now. (*He gets up and goes into the kitchen.*)

MARY. (*following him, half upset, half amused*) No, Philip, don't be silly, we can't have a boarded up door in our kitchen. Sooner or later we're going to need to go down there for something. What if we need an embalming bottle? (*He opens the cupboard, takes out the boards, nails and a hammer.*) Philip, you are NOT going to board up the basement door.

PHILIP. So you're going down to have a look, then?

MARY. No, let's just go back to bed, some other night—

PHILIP. Fine, I'll just be a minute, boarding it up, and then we can go to bed and make love.

MARY. No.

PHILIP. No, we're not going to make love?

MARY. No, I'm not going to let you board up the basement door.

PHILIP. Well, make up your mind, Mary. Are you going down to have a look or aren't you? It's up to you.

MARY. All right, all right, I'll go down.

PHILIP. Okay. Well, I'm glad we've settled that. I take a great deal of comfort in knowing where I stand.

MARY. Philip, I know I've been acting a little strangely, lately, but—

PHILIP. Go on, you'll be late.

MARY. I really don't hear anything tonight. I'd rather just stay up here with you. (*She begins to caress him.*) You could do it to me here in the kitchen, with the lights on, or the lights off, on the floor, against the wall, we could explore all kinds of possibilities here, Philip—

PHILIP. We could do it on the table.

MARY. All right.

PHILIP. I could spray whipped cream on your breasts and then lick it off.

MARY. Oh, I'd like that.

PHILIP. We have butterscotch pudding.

MARY. Yes, we do.

PHILIP. I could smear it all over your stomach and your thighs and then eat it.

SOMETHING IN THE BASEMENT   33

MARY. Oh, let's do that, yes.

PHILIP. You'd like that?

MARY. I'd love it, Philip, let's do that right now.

PHILIP. All right. I'll just board up the basement door first, and then we can get right to it.

MARY. I don't understand why you've got to—

PHILIP. Because it's got to be one or the other, Mary. You can't have both. Pick what you want, but you can't have both. I've thought this all through, and you can choose what you please, but you can't have it both ways, do you understand that? (*Pause. She looks at him.*)

MARY. All right. I'll go down and have a look. But I won't stay. I'll just have a look, and I'll come right back up to you, and then we'll make love, and everything will be all right. You're different now, you're not so safe, I'm not sure about you, I don't know when you're kidding and when you're not, I don't know what you're going to do from one moment to the next. I like that. That's very attractive. In a fatal kind of way. I'm trembling. (*She kisses him, a very erotic kiss.*) I'll just be a minute. (*She takes the flashlight, smiles at him a little uncertainly, and goes down the steps. PHILIP stands motionless. He listens. Then, faintly, the tinkling sound, like wind chimes, and the shuffling noise. Faint sound of gentle laughter from MARY below. Another laugh. PHILIP closes the basement door carefully. Then he picks up the hammer. Hesitates. He opens the door again, hammer in hand. Another soft laugh from MARY. He closes the door. Then he picks up a board and some nails and begins to board up the door.*) Philip? (*He continues to hammer, quietly, methodically, very efficiently.*) Philip? What are you doing? (*His pounding is becoming gradually faster and harder as he adds more boards.*) What is this? Is this some sort of erotic game? I love games. Games are exciting. Philip? (*The door is being rapidly covered with boards. PHILIP pounds faster and harder.*) Philip? You're going to let me out, aren't you? Philip? Let me out now. Philip? PHILIP? PHILIP?

(*He is pounding frantically. Lights fade and go out.*)

Scarecrow

CHARACTERS:

Cally, 18
Rose, 36
Nick, 27

SETTING:

Four wooden chairs on a bare stage.
All three characters are present all the time. They move about in the course of the play and relate to each other in various ways, but they do not act out or mime in any way the actions they describe as they speak.

Scarecrow began as an experimental video project, and was shot on location in and around a farm near Iowa City, Iowa in the summer of 1979, with the following cast:

ROSE	Carmel Quinn
CALLY	Judith Zeiler
NICK	John Fisher

It was directed by Diane Troyer.

Scarecrow

(*Lights up slowly on three people. ROSE is very attractive, wears a simple cotton dress, as does her daughter, CALLY, who is quite beautiful. NICK wears bluejeans and a flannel shirt.*)

CALLY. In the cornfield next to our house there's a scarecrow, it's been there as long as I can remember, and it's always frightened me. When I walk through the corn to the creek in the summer I don't like to look at him, but the thing seems to draw me. You can hear the sound of the crows in the afternoon. The stillness, the rustling of the corn, the feel of broken earth under my bare feet, one hawk drifting high in a blue sky. Out in the cornfield, away from the house, my body is alive.

ROSE. What are you dreaming about?

CALLY. Do you want some cereal, Mama?

ROSE. I hate cereal.

CALLY. You don't hate cereal.

ROSE. I hate anything that crunches when you bite into it. It's like roaches in milk.

CALLY. You like cornflakes.

ROSE. I don't eat corn. And we're out of milk.

CALLY. We've got milk.

ROSE. Our milk's gone bad.

CALLY. I got it fresh from Mr. Pritchard yesterday.

ROSE. I didn't know Mr. Pritchard gave milk.

CALLY. His cow gives milk.

ROSE. I thought they had a bull.

CALLY. He's got both, Mama, that's how we get little baby cows.

ROSE. Yes, and it's a big mistake.

CALLY. Do you want cornflakes or don't you?

ROSE. I don't feel good. I can't breathe.

CALLY. You don't feel good in the morning because you don't eat.

ROSE. I don't eat because I don't feel good.

CALLY. Well, no wonder.

ROSE. I used to feel good in the morning.

CALLY. It must have been before I was born.

ROSE. Yes, as a matter of fact, it was.

CALLY. Well, I'm sorry, Mama, if I'd known in the womb I was going to depress you this much and ruin your breakfast, I'd have thought twice about coming out.

ROSE. You never thought twice in your life.

CALLY. Eat this.

ROSE. Eat it yourself.

CALLY. Why can't you eat regular meals like normal people?

ROSE. Why do you care whether I eat breakfast or not? Are you keeping score? You saving boxtops for a trip to Disneyland?

CALLY. If you don't eat, you're going to die.

ROSE. Good.

CALLY. Maybe you could breathe better if you went outside once in a while, did you ever think of that?

ROSE. I go outside.

CALLY. When was the last time you went into town?

ROSE. Why would I want to go into town?

CALLY. When was the last time you went anyplace?

ROSE. I was out on the porch Thursday. I think it was Thursday. Maybe it was Wednesday.

CALLY. I don't mean on the porch.

ROSE. You said outside. The porch is outside.

CALLY. Mama, you're in pretty bad shape if your big event of the year is a trip out onto the porch.

ROSE. I've got everything I need right here. I've got my

books and pictures and my writing and my piano and a wonderful collection of National Geographics.

CALLY. What more could a girl ask for.

ROSE. I don't know.

CALLY. Mama, a person needs to go outside for things once in a while, you know?

ROSE. That's what I've got you for.

CALLY. Lucky me.

ROSE. What?

CALLY. Just eat your cornflakes.

ROSE. You got something in your craw, spit it out.

CALLY. Mama, what if maybe sometime I wasn't always here?

ROSE. You're always here.

CALLY. But what if I wasn't?

ROSE. You planning on running away from me, is that what this conversation is about? You gonna run off and join the circus? Goin to Columbus to be a model and pose naked on top of automobiles? I see you looking at yourself in the mirror all the time. I know. I used to look like that.

CALLY. You still do. You look nice.

ROSE. I'm old.

CALLY. That's stupid, you're thirty-six, Mama, you're a lot younger than lots of those women on television, you'd look just great if you took any care of yourself at all, instead of poking around like an old lady in your National Geographics and trying to write some stupid book. What do you think you're doing with your life? You've got to start taking care of yourself again.

ROSE. For what?

CALLY. For if something should happen to me.

ROSE. Nothing's going to happen to you.

CALLY. But what if something does? What if by accident some day something should actually, unexpectedly, finally happen to me?

ROSE. Like what?

CALLY. I don't know. Something you didn't plan on when you got up in the morning.

ROSE. Nothing is going to happen.

CALLY. That's what I'm afraid of.

ROSE. So are you planning on running off and leaving me or aren't you?

CALLY. I don't know.

ROSE. Promise me you won't do that.

CALLY. I don't want to promise you.

ROSE. Promise, I want you to promise.

CALLY. Let me alone.

ROSE. I bet you got it all planned.

CALLY. No I don't.

ROSE. Then why won't you promise?

CALLY. I just don't want to.

ROSE. Why is it so hard to promise?

CALLY. I won't promise you I'm going to stay here in this house and rot for the rest of my life, I just can't.

ROSE. Then eat your breakfast. You want to be a pinup girl, you better put some meat on your bones.

CALLY. I'm not hungry.

ROSE. You're too skinny.

CALLY. So are you. Models are skinny.

ROSE. So you do want to pose naked in them magazines.

CALLY. Yes, Mama, I want to pose stark naked for National Geographic, maybe I could be eaten by a Polar Bear or something, I think that would be real exciting, don't you?

ROSE. Maybe for the bear.

NICK. I can hear them fighting in the house. I stand in

the corn and listen to their voices. The house is a kind of womb. I wait for it to give birth.

CALLY. This is the geography of the house. It's an old farmhouse. There is a kitchen, a sitting room, two bedrooms upstairs, a front porch with a swing. In the sitting room there is an old upright piano with photographs and sheet music on it. A rocking chair, a soft chair with a footstool, an old sofa. Mother has a large bed with many pictures. In the kitchen there is a very old sink and refrigerator, an old stove, a round wooden table with highbacked old chairs, a wooden cabinet with glass doors full of cups and dishes, an old desk with a bowl of fruit. Clocks everywhere, ticking. They all say different times. It's always cool in the house. Sometimes I feel safe there. Sometimes I feel trapped, like in a coffin.

ROSE. Where have you been?

CALLY. No place.

ROSE. Where did you go?

CALLY. I was here, I'm always here.

ROSE. You stay out of that cornfield, it don't belong to us.

CALLY. Nobody cares if I walk over there.

ROSE. I care. You just stay out of there.

CALLY. My God, can't I even take a walk once in a while?

ROSE. I don't want to argue about it.

CALLY. Then don't.

ROSE. What do you do out there in that cornfield?

CALLY. Nothing.

ROSE. Play around with the corncobs?

CALLY. I wouldn't have to walk if I had a car.

ROSE. You gonna drive a car through the cornfield?

CALLY. No, I'd drive to Disneyland.

ROSE. I gave you a car.

CALLY. You gave me a Studebaker.

ROSE. That's a car.

CALLY. It doesn't run.

ROSE. You got to put gas in it.

CALLY. It's been sittin out there in the barn with chicken shit all over it for twenty years, I can't drive that.

ROSE. You drive my car.

CALLY. Into town, once a week, to the grocery store and the post office and once a month to the bank, and if I'm not back in a half hour you call the police.

ROSE. That's their job, to find missing persons, they enjoy it.

CALLY. I need a car of my own that runs.

ROSE. Then buy one.

CALLY. I don't have any money.

ROSE. That's not my fault.

CALLY. You won't let me get a job.

ROSE. I need you here.

CALLY. What for?

ROSE. Lots of things.

CALLY. There's Grandma's money.

ROSE. I ain't wastin your grandmother's money buyin you a car you don't need so you can get a job you don't want and disappear on me.

NICK. At night the women sleep in their beds and the clocks tick and the stillness is broken by owls. The girl is dreaming about me, she moves her legs and moans in her sleep. The mother watches from the doorway and says nothing. In the morning the light creeps in through the blinds and touches the girl's naked body.

ROSE. Where's my glasses? I lost my glasses.

CALLY. You don't need glasses.

ROSE. Don't tell me if I need glasses or not. Find my glasses.

CALLY. All right, I'll look for them.

ROSE. Not in my room. Stay out of my room. I don't want you pokin around in my things.

CALLY. Then get new glasses.

ROSE. I don't need new glasses, I've got my old glasses.

CALLY. I can't find them.

ROSE. Did you look in my room?

CALLY. I'm not allowed in your room. Why don't YOU look in your room?

ROSE. Because I don't have my glasses.

CALLY. They'll turn up in a year or two.

ROSE. I could be dead in a year or two.

CALLY. Then you won't need glasses.

ROSE. Don't sit there and pout, you're not old enough to have a car.

CALLY. I'm eighteen.

ROSE. I know what happens in cars. Them boys used to come around here after you all the time, with them cars. They should all go out and run over each other, which thank God they do.

CALLY. They were just boys from school. They liked me. They were my friends.

ROSE. Boys don't like a person, Cally, and they don't want to be friends with you, they want to DO things to you.

CALLY. They were nice boys, most of them.

ROSE. If they were so damn nice, where are they now, if they liked you so much?

CALLY. Mama, if I was them I'd stop comin around, too, if some crazy woman shot buckshot at me every time I pulled up to the house. You could have killed somebody.

ROSE. Yes, but I didn't have my glasses.

CALLY. They didn't mean any harm.

ROSE. Of course they meant harm. What do you think they wanted to do? Teach you a foreign language? Boys is all sex, and all sex does is make more sex, more little wet things that grow up stupid and make more sex.

CALLY. That's just life.

ROSE. Well, I'm against it. Here in this one National Geographic I found this article on Antarctica, where it's all snow and ice, nothin much else but a few penguins, maybe, just cold, everyplace. That's south, you know, not north. So far south that it's cold. There's a lesson there. You go too far into the heat and you find the cold.

CALLY. You're insane, you know that, Mama?

ROSE. That's where I want to go. So far south that it's cold. All white. No crows. No cornfields. Dead places, waste places, cold. (*pause*) The clock stopped.

CALLY. Which one? How can you tell? You keep them all running at different times, and with the radio broke and the television broke, we ain't never gonna know what time it is.

ROSE. I don't care what time it is, I just like to hear all my little friends go tick tick tick.

CALLY. I'm going for a walk.

ROSE. Stay here and do the dishes.

CALLY. There aren't any dishes.

ROSE. I got a coffee cup here.

CALLY. There's coffee in it, Mama, you want me to put dishwater in your coffee?

ROSE. Tastes like you already did.

CALLY. I'll wash it later, I'm just going to take a walk.

ROSE. You go out that door, it's gonna be locked when you try and get back in.

CALLY. It doesn't lock.

ROSE. I'll nail it shut.

CALLY. I'm just going outside for a while, I can't breathe in here.

ROSE. You stay in this house with me, it's gonna rain. (*pause*) There she goes, always slams the screen door, that's my girl. Wind the clock. Time run, nobody can help it. Gonna happen soon, now. Wait eighteen years, and then it comes. Just keep your gun loaded. Scarecrow come to Mama. I can smell the son of a bitch on her clothes. She's ripe, oh yes, she's a ripe one. He's gonna plow that field. Down at the center of the end of the world, far south, in the white, God lives there, frozen. I can smell the smell on her clothes. Time of rut.

CALLY. You always know, don't you? Before I get here. Before you turn around to look at me. You know I'm here.

NICK. Who else would it be?

CALLY. Did you miss me yesterday?

NICK. Didn't you come yesterday?

CALLY. You know I didn't. She wouldn't let me.

NICK. I don't see how she could stop you, if you really wanted to come.

CALLY. I'm sure she thinks I'm meeting somebody out here.

NICK. Well, she's right, isn't she?

CALLY. She thinks it's something dirty. She doesn't understand about people being just friends. I mean, without sex or anything.

NICK. Is there no sex?

CALLY. We don't have sex.

NICK. Don't we?

CALLY. No. We talk.

NICK. What do we talk about?

CALLY. You know what we talk about. We talk about everything.

NICK. If we talk about everything, we must talk about sex. What kind of a girl meets a strange man every day on the other side of a cornfield to talk about sex?

CALLY. You're teasing me.

NICK. Sex is different things. (*pause*)

CALLY. Maybe you should come to the house and meet her, and just get it over with. Maybe I could just invite you to the house for dinner or something, and you could charm her to death.

NICK. I've been there.

CALLY. To the house? No you haven't.

NICK. Yes I have.

CALLY. When?

NICK. I saw in your window.

CALLY. Really?

NICK. Yes.

CALLY. You saw me?

NICK. Yes, it was you.

CALLY. When did you see me?

NICK. Last night.

CALLY. Why?

NICK. Because you didn't come.

CALLY. You looked in the window? Of our house?

NICK. I was worried.

CALLY. Why didn't you knock on the door?

NICK. I didn't know if I was welcome.

CALLY. What did you see? What was I doing?

NICK. Looking at yourself in the mirror.

CALLY. You were spying on me.

NICK. You used to spy on me all the time, before you got up the courage to come over and talk to me.

CALLY. No I didn't. Well, maybe I did, but that was different. I was just looking in the mirror? That's all?

NICK. You were touching the tips of your breasts.

CALLY. No I wasn't.

NICK. Yes you were. Touching your nipples with your fingertips.

CALLY. You saw me naked? You looked through my window and saw me naked?

NICK. No. I'm just teasing you. I wouldn't do that. Why, is that what you do? Touch yourself and look in the mirror?

CALLY. You're horrible.

NICK. I'm not horrible.

CALLY. Yes you are.

NICK. You watched me swimming in the crick that time, didn't you?

CALLY. I never.

NICK. Yes you did.

CALLY. That's an entirely different thing.

NICK. Why is it different?

CALLY. Because you're a man.

NICK. So?

CALLY. It's just different. You're not supposed to see my breasts until I want you to.

NICK. And you don't want me to see your breasts.

CALLY. Not through the window. Maybe some time.

NICK. You're afraid of me.

CALLY. No I'm not.

NICK. You ran from me, the first time I turned around and looked at you. You ran through that corn like the devil was after you.

CALLY. I like to run. I run with my eyes closed and the corn hits me in the face and the body, my body just churning inside, heart just ready to explode. I feel safe. Scared, but safe. Like with you. Like when I'm with you.

NICK. Then why did you let your mother bully you into staying home yesterday?

CALLY. You better be careful, looking in our windows, she might catch you.

NICK. No she won't.

CALLY. She will. She's not stupid.
NICK. What if she does catch me? What then?
CALLY. She has a gun.
NICK. Come over here.
CALLY. I can't stay today, I've got to get back.
NICK. Come here.
CALLY. Why?
NICK. I want to see your breasts.
CALLY. I don't think you should.
NICK. Yes you do.
CALLY. Nick.
ROSE. Where the hell have you been?
CALLY. Just takin a walk.
ROSE. You been in that cornfield again.
CALLY. What if I have? You been spyin on me?
ROSE. I've got a right to look out my own windows.
CALLY. And what did you see, when you looked out your windows?
ROSE. I saw enough.
CALLY. You couldn't see anything, you didn't have your glasses.
ROSE. You're not going out there any more.
CALLY. You've got nothing to say about it.
ROSE. There's work to do here.
CALLY. I do my work.
ROSE. I could be dead in here for all you care.
CALLY. I'm not going to spend all my time locked up in this house with you.
ROSE. You hate me, don't you?
CALLY. I don't hate you.
ROSE. You'd be a lot happier if I was dead.
CALLY. I'd be happier if you'd just let me alone once in a while.
ROSE. I raised you up from nothing. Took care of you,

no husband to help me. You've got nothing but me. And I've got nothing but you. There's not a thing out there you need. Go to town and they take your money. Meet a man and he takes your body and uses it. Have a child and she sucks out your love and spits it in the dirt. There's nothing out there for you.

CALLY. I don't think you know anything about what's out there.

ROSE. I been out there.

CALLY. That was a long time ago.

ROSE. It doesn't change. It changes, but it doesn't change. I read in the National Geographic that out in the south sea islands they still eat people pretty regular. Life is the same everywhere.

NICK. So how's your mother today? Cheerful as ever?

CALLY. Why are you always so interested in my mother?

NICK. I'm interested in everything you're interested in.

CALLY. I'm not interested in my mother. She doesn't interest me at all.

NICK. Yes she does.

CALLY. My mother is in great need of something, I'm not sure what. She's a beautiful woman, she was my age when she had me, but she acts like an old person, and she has trouble breathing, she says it's her heart or asthma or something, and she stays in the house all day playing the piano and writing her book.

NICK. She's writing a book?

CALLY. Yes.

NICK. About what?

CALLY. About evil, I think. About what evil is.

NICK. And does your mother know? What evil is?

CALLY. I guess she thinks she does.

NICK. Maybe you should think more about yourself and less about your mother.

CALLY. What about myself?

NICK. What are you going to do with your life?

CALLY. I try not to think about that, that only depresses me. I don't think I'm going to do anything with it.

NICK. What would you be, if you had your choice?

CALLY. I don't know. I'd travel. I'd want to see things.

NICK. Good. Go and do it.

CALLY. I can't.

NICK. Why can't you?

CALLY. Because I've got to take care of my mother.

NICK. Might do her good to be on her own for a while.

CALLY. But what if something happened to her while I was gone?

NICK. What's going to happen?

CALLY. She really isn't well.

NICK. You don't think she just tells you that to keep you home?

CALLY. No.

NICK. How sure are you?

CALLY. I think we should talk about something else.

NICK. She's thirty-six, right? She could live to be fifty, sixty, seventy, eighty. How would you like to live here fifty more years with her?

CALLY. Don't say that. That's awful.

NICK. If you're going to stay here until she dies, and you don't want to stay here, then it follows that you'd better hope she dies young, or you're going to lose all your teeth before you get out of here.

CALLY. I don't want to listen to this sort of talk.

NICK. You don't want to listen to it because it's true.

CALLY. I know it's true. I just don't want to listen to it. (*pause*) She's going to live to be a hundred and twenty, I know it, I just know it. (*pause*)

NICK. You have the most beautiful legs. I love to rub my hands along your legs. Your legs feel so good against the palms of my hands.

ROSE. Just who do you think you're fooling, girl?

CALLY. I don't know what you mean.

ROSE. You been seein somebody out there.

CALLY. Who would I see?

ROSE. Some man. You been seein some man.

CALLY. Would it be such a terrible thing if I was?

ROSE. It might be.

CALLY. Don't you want me to have any friends, ever?

ROSE. A man is not a friend. You think I'm stupid enough to believe a man can be a friend?

CALLY. I'm tired. I'm going to bed.

ROSE. I can tell by the way you act, Cally.

CALLY. Am I not supposed to talk to any man, ever?

ROSE. I can't think of any good reason to.

CALLY. I can.

ROSE. You got to stay away from them, like me.

CALLY. You've talked to men.

ROSE. Nope.

CALLY. You must have talked to my father, at least.

ROSE. I'd have been a lot better off if I hadn't.

CALLY. You wouldn't have ME if you hadn't.

ROSE. And I'd be a lot better off.

CALLY. If that's what you think of me, then why do you care what I do?

ROSE. I just don't want you going out there and meeting a man in that cornfield.

CALLY. I am going to do exactly what I please.

ROSE. You stay in this house or I'll beat you black and blue.

CALLY. You just try it.

ROSE. I will, see if I don't.

CALLY. You hit me and I'll hit you back.

ROSE. You'd hit your mother, would you?

CALLY. You'd hit me, why can't I hit you?

ROSE. You are a terrible, dirty, debased girl, with no feelings, no morals, and what's more, you're stupid.

CALLY. Who made me who I am? I'm not stupid and I do have feelings and if there's anything wrong with me, there's nobody to blame but you. You made me.

ROSE. You don't have any idea what made you, and if you're lucky, you never will, and you can thank God, and me, for that.

CALLY. What is that supposed to mean?

ROSE. You'll see. Keep it up and you'll see.

CALLY. Are you talking about my father? Because I don't want to hear you saying any more bad things about my father, do you hear me?

ROSE. What do you know about it?

CALLY. I know he ran off and left you, and if I was him, I'd probably have done the same thing, I certainly don't blame him for it.

ROSE. I've raised an ingrate and a fool.

CALLY. I don't care what you think of me, I'll go where I please and I'll do just what I like, and if you don't care for that, Mama, you can just go somewhere and die. You're hateful and selfish and I wish you'd just die.

ROSE. All right then. Why don't you invite him over to the house.

CALLY. What?

ROSE. If you feel this strongly about him, why don't you just invite your young man over here for dinner? Have him over. I'd like to see him. I'd like to meet him. Invite him over for dinner, why don't you?

CALLY. So you can scream at him and drive him away like you did everybody else?

ROSE. Ask him over.

CALLY. You go to hell, Mama. Just go to hell.
ROSE. Get back here.
CALLY. No.
ROSE. Yes, run off. Run to him now. You hate me. It's sad, but it's the only way. You think you understand, but you don't understand anything, poor child, not yet. But you will. Soon you will.
CALLY. I hate her. I just hate her. I don't know what I'm going to do. I can't live like this. I thought for a minute she was going to kill me.
NICK. Why don't you just leave?
CALLY. Because I've got no place to go.
NICK. There must be some place.
CALLY. No. There isn't.
NICK. Relatives?
CALLY. Nobody I know, not that well, just her people, and they'd all side with her, probably, even though they don't like her much, either. And I never knew any of my father's people. I don't even know if he HAD any people.
NICK. What about friends?
CALLY. She drove away all my friends.
NICK. You want to come with me? We could run off.
CALLY. Don't tease me.
NICK. I'm not teasing you. Come with me.
CALLY. She'd never let me.
NICK. Don't tell her.
CALLY. I promised her I'd stay with her.
NICK. You don't have to keep a promise she bullied you into.
CALLY. I don't have any money.
NICK. That's okay. Neither do I.
CALLY. How would we live? How do you live now?
NICK. I get by.
CALLY. How?

NICK. I do odd jobs.

CALLY. Where? Not on your cabin. It's falling apart. It's so bad you won't even let me in there.

NICK. That's just a place I sleep. I don't do odd jobs for myself. I do them for other people.

CALLY. What kind of odd jobs?

NICK. Different things. Some jobs odder than others. I worked in the mines for a while. Deep in the ground. You go deep enough into the earth and it starts to get very warm. I liked the mines.

CALLY. I don't think I want to work in a mine.

NICK. She's got money, doesn't she?

CALLY. What makes you think that?

NICK. You must live off something.

CALLY. There's money from my grandmother. She left it for me when she died. Mama was pregnant with me then. She keeps it hidden, in a box in her room. My mother doesn't believe in banks, except to cash the checks she gets in the mail. She gets checks for something, I don't know what they are, she's got stock in some company or something, my grandmother left that, too.

NICK. If your grandmother left it for you, then it isn't your mother's money, it's your money.

CALLY. I guess so.

NICK. Then why don't you just take it?

CALLY. I can't take her money.

NICK. You just said it was YOUR money.

CALLY. I couldn't do that.

NICK. You deserve to have a life. You wouldn't be stealing from her. She's been stealing from you. She's stealing your future, and your happiness. She's stealing your soul. Take it back, it belongs to you.

CALLY. I don't think I could just run off with the

money and leave her. I can't just forget about her. She's my mother.

NICK. You're a grown up girl, you can do whatever you want.

CALLY. She'd call the police and have me arrested. She would, I know she would. I wish I was dead.

NICK. No you don't. You wish SHE was dead. (*pause*) I don't care. It's none of my business. Do what you please. I don't think I'm going to be around here much longer, anyway.

CALLY. I think what I want is for you to make love to me. (*pause*)

ROSE. Out in the cornfield waiting, always been, feet all twisted like claws, your eyes are burning, I know you, seen you smile at me a thousand times, scarecrow's brain, bugs crawling inside, flies around your mouth, scarecrow grin, straw man, lurk in the dark in the cornfield, full moon eater, bringer of sex and death, I've heard you whisper to me, felt you in the night, your cold breath makes me shudder, whisper poetry and filth. You think you got her now, the evil in us makes it easy for you, but there is also what is stubborn in her, that loves me, that will turn on you when it makes no sense to, hate and love and lust keep her running, ticking like a clock, flesh and blood like twisted watches, I know what you are, I remember, I feel it, the red scarecrow eyes through the long rows of corn like mourners watching, rustling quiet in the breeze, dead thing, lives on the hate, in the dirt. You are going to burn like my loins. I'm going to burn you. I've baited you a little trap, my love. Love kills. Love always kills. I love you still. I smell death on your clothes. I rock in my chair and wait for you to come to me, smelling of death like bread baking in the afternoon.

CALLY. I've got to go home now. It's late, it's so late, I don't know what got into me, I just couldn't leave you, I just couldn't separate my skin from you, but I got to go now, it's so late, she's going to kill me, she is, she really is, this time.

NICK. She's not going to kill you.

CALLY. She'll make me wish I was dead. She'll talk to me like she was stabbing me with knives.

NICK. Why do you care what she says to you?

CALLY. When I was a little girl she was so good, she was so good, I loved her, she was very warm, and funny, and good to me, and she was always there, and she would hold me, and talk to me, and teach me things, and comfort me. But when I started to grow up, she began to change, like she was waiting for something, like she was being cruel to me, on purpose, for some reason, something she was waiting for. She breathes so hard at night when she's asleep, I can hear her from my room, and I think, what if she stops breathing? What would I do? And she talks to herself, in her sleep, and when she's awake, all the time.

NICK. What does she talk about?

CALLY. Cornfields and scarecrows, snatches of stuff about my father, crazy things, I don't know.

NICK. What does she say about your father?

CALLY. She hates him.

NICK. After all this time?

CALLY. I think so. I think it's hate. It's something like hate.

NICK. She felt differently about him once, though.

CALLY. I guess she must have. I'm afraid to go back. I don't want to go back there.

NICK. For all you know, this could be the night she finally stops breathing. She might just take a breath and then not take another one, and solve all your problems.

CALLY. No. That's not going to happen.

NICK. You know, Cally, if I was as sick and unhappy as your mother, maybe I'd rather stop breathing. I mean, maybe that's what all this cranky behavior is really about. Maybe she's just tired of living. Maybe what she'd really like is, next time she has trouble breathing at night, maybe if you'd just put a pillow very tenderly over her face and help her stop breathing, maybe she'd be happier.

CALLY. That would be nice. Then we could take my grandmother's money and run off and nobody would bother us.

NICK. Maybe. (*pause*)

CALLY. Too bad I would never really do a thing like that.

NICK. Yes. Too bad. (*pause*) Well, I've got to be moving along pretty soon, one way or the other, anyway.

CALLY. Moving along to where?

NICK. I don't know. I'll find out when I get there, I guess.

CALLY. When?

NICK. Maybe tonight.

CALLY. You're joking, aren't you? You wouldn't really go.

NICK. I'm not sure there's anything for me around here.

CALLY. What about me?

NICK. You want to come along?

CALLY. Where?

NICK. Anyplace you like. Of course, it might be kind of rough. Unless you could come up with some money somewhere.

CALLY. I don't want you to leave me.

NICK. I don't want to leave you, but, really, what's the point?

CALLY. Don't go.

NICK. You better go home.

CALLY. Before you leave, come to the house. Come to the house later, before you leave, will you promise me you'll stop at the house?

NICK. If you like.

CALLY. Promise.

NICK. All right. I promise. (*pause*)

CALLY. On the way back to the house it's dark, and I move through the corn like a ghost, making a wide circle around where I know the scarecrow is, I don't want him looking at me, the fear from my childhood is still inside me, the cool night touches my flesh. I step into the house and everything is dark except a small light in the kitchen. My mother has gone to bed. The ticking clocks. The sound of her breathing in her sleep, forced, troubled. I go up the steps to her bedroom and look in. She is very beautiful, sleeping there, but she breathes so hard. Very carefully I stoop down and reach under the bed, and there is an old wooden chocolate box, and inside the box is the money, so much money there. She seems to be having a nightmare. She is so unhappy. Maybe I could make us both happy. Maybe I could end her misery and mine. It would be so easy. I could just take the pillow there beside her and softly lay it over her face. It would be the easiest thing in the world. Nobody would know. It would be an act of love. I take the pillow in my hands. I put it back. Then I take it again. My heart is pounding. I can't breathe. The pillow is almost touching her. It is almost touching her lips. Then her eyes open.

ROSE. Just what the hell do you think you're doing?

CALLY. Uh, I uh, I thought you might, I was just, I thought you might, I was, you, uh —

ROSE. You thought you were going to get rid of me,

didn't you? You thought old Mom would be better company dead, is that right?

CALLY. No.

ROSE. Bury old Mom in the garden under the petunias, is that about it, huh?

CALLY. I don't know what you mean, I was just—

ROSE. I see you been countin my money there for me, haven't you?

CALLY. Mama, I'm sorry, don't hurt me, I didn't mean it, I just—

ROSE. He put you up to this, didn't he? He put you up to it, I know he did.

CALLY. I'm sorry, I wouldn't hurt you, I just, I don't know, I just—Mama, I can't live like this, I can't—

ROSE. I knew. I knew all along you'd come in here some day and do that. I knew.

CALLY. How could you know? You couldn't know. I'm so sorry—

ROSE. Oh, listen, you stop blubberin and listen to me. You meet him out by that beech tree on the other side of the cornfield, by the crick, isn't that right?

CALLY. How do you know that?

ROSE. How do you think I know?

CALLY. You followed me? You saw us?

ROSE. No, I didn't follow you, I didn't have to.

CALLY. What have you got? High powered binoculars?

ROSE. I know because when I was a girl just your age I met him out there, on the other side of the cornfield, under the beech tree by the crick, and he said he loved me, and he made love to me, and he sent me in here to kill your grandmother, just like he sent you here tonight, but she ran away from me into that cornfield and I found her dead underneath that scarecrow.

CALLY. Mama, that wasn't him, that was somebody else, the man I meet out there is only a few years older than I am, he's a young man, Mama.

ROSE. He's as old or young as he wants to be and he's a lover makes you crazy, I know all about it, I'm tellin you, Cally.

CALLY. I don't understand what you're saying.

ROSE. I'm saying he was my lover before he was yours.

CALLY. You never did. Not with him.

ROSE. I was a virgin girl like you was when I met him out under that beech tree, and I never touched a man after.

CALLY. Mama, that's crazy, you're crazy.

ROSE. He's afraid to come into this house, isn't he?

CALLY. No.

ROSE. Then why hasn't he been to the house? Why hasn't he come into the house, then?

CALLY. Because I didn't want you shootin him full of buckshot, that's why.

ROSE. No, it's because there's a Bible in this house, and he's afraid of it, so he draws you out to the cornfield, he don't live in that cabin like he told you, there's nothin in that old cabin, he lives in the scarecrow, he's alive inside the scarecrow, and he's been waiting all these years for his little girl to grow up.

CALLY. Mama, I'm going to call you a doctor, right now, you're ready for the funny farm.

ROSE. You got to save us from him. You got to go out into that cornfield and burn down that scarecrow. The evil is in the scarecrow, you've got to burn it.

CALLY. Just calm down, you're going to have a seizure or something.

ROSE. Burn it, you got to burn it tonight.

CALLY. You're crazy.

SCARECROW 61

ROSE. All right, fine, I'm crazy, then it won't do any harm to just humor me and go out there and burn that thing, now, will it?

CALLY. Why don't you do it?

ROSE. I tried, lots of times, but I ain't strong enough, it's too evil, I can't get near enough to it, it makes me all weak and sick and I can't breathe when I get near it, it's got to be somebody young and strong like you, it'll fight you, you got to do it for me, just this one thing, I made you strong and cruel so you could do this for me, go on, burn it.

CALLY. Mama, I'm not going to go out there and burn down some scarecrow, now, and that's all there is to it.

ROSE. You take the kitchen matches and go out and burn that scarecrow, and if you do that, I'll give you all the money I got, all the money you was going to take after you killed me, and you can go anywhere you please and do anything you please, I swear, I won't try and stop you, but you got to burn that scarecrow for me first. That's all you got to do.

CALLY. I don't want to.

ROSE. You're scared of it, I know, you always was, ever since you was little, but you got to, there's nobody else but you, you got to do it.

CALLY. I can't.

ROSE. What's the matter, Cally? You scared it's true?

CALLY. No.

ROSE. Then go and do it. Prove I'm crazy. Prove I'm wrong. Go and burn that scarecrow. Burn it and you can have everything. Take the matches. Take them. That's my girl. I knew you would. Go on. Good girl. Go on.

CALLY. Why not? Why shouldn't I? It's just an old scarecrow. It's made of straw and burlap and old clothes stuffed with straw. It's there to scare the blackbirds and the crows. That's all it is. All I have to do is take out a match and light it and I'll be free. I'll have the money and I'll be free. Then I can go away with my lover and I'll be free. Except. Except that it keeps looking at me. Don't look at me. Why does it keep looking at me? I've seen it smile at me as I went by. Once on a hot day I took off my clothes and lay down naked in the sun and I could feel it watching me, through the cornstalks. It smiled. It's smiling now. Stop that. I'm shaking, my body is shaking. Are those my father's clothes you're wearing? Is that my father's smile? Don't watch me take the match out of the box. I'm going to burn you. I'm going to burn you now. I'm going to burn you all up. I am. The match will light. It will light. Why is the match so difficult to light? Why am I shaking like this? I'm sweating. My legs are shaking. I'm not going to faint. You're not going to stop me. I'm going away with my lover and you can't stop me. He isn't you. He's real, he's flesh and blood, I know he's flesh and blood because he's touched every part of me, he's been inside me, he loves me, why won't the matches light, why won't they light?

ROSE. Do it.

NICK. She can't do it.

CALLY. Another match. I'll try another match. Another match. I'm sick, I feel sick, it's like somebody is whispering in my head, somebody is touching me, touching me, like a whisp of straw, oh, God, oh, God, I can feel his hands on me. Calm down. Nothing will light. It's not you that's doing this. It's me. My hands won't work. My hands won't work. Help me. I'm going to burn you.

ROSE. Do it, Cally, please, please.

NICK. She can't. She can't do it.

CALLY. Mama, I don't think I can.

ROSE. You can. Just take the match, just light the match. Don't look at it. Don't look at it. Just light the match.

NICK. You can't, Cally.

CALLY. I can't. He keeps looking at me. Why does he keep looking at me? He's laughing at me, Mama, make him stop laughing at me. I can't breathe. I can't breathe.

ROSE. Give me the matches.

CALLY. No. Let him alone. Don't.

ROSE. Give me the matches. It's got to be done. It hurts in my chest. Give me the matches.

CALLY. Stop it, Mama, you're getting too upset, don't.

ROSE. I'll do it this time. I'll do it this time.

CALLY. Mama.

NICK. She can't do it either.

CALLY. Mama, don't, please.

ROSE. Don't listen to him, don't listen to him, you got to make yourself deaf to it, he'll talk to you and touch you and talk to you and touch you and talk to you and touch you. I can't breathe. Why won't the matches light? Why won't the matches light? I can't breathe. Pick up the matches. Pick up the matches. Pick up the matches. (*pause*)

NICK. Cally?

CALLY. I live in the house alone now. I remember a time when I wanted to go, but I can't remember why. I read my Bible and my magazines and rock in my rocking chair, and feel the child growing inside my womb. I can feel her growing in my womb.

NICK. Cally?

CALLY. He comes at night and calls to me from outside, he calls to me, but I won't listen to him. He says it's his little girl I've got growing inside me, and he begs me to come outside, but I won't. I won't go outside. He's afraid to come into the house. I will raise my little girl. I will teach her to be strong and cruel. And I will teach her what to do. And this time, we'll get him.

(The three people are motionless. Fade to darkness, ticking clocks.)

Lurker

CHARACTERS:

Marston, a man in his thirties
Lil, a woman in her twenties

SETTING:

A garden.

Lurker was produced in New York in March and April, 1987 at the Nat Horne Theatre by the Manhattan Class Company, Will Cantler and Pat Skipper, producers. It featured Mary B. Ward and later Leila Kenzle as Lil, and Robert LuPone as Marston. Directed by Roy B. Steinberg. Stage Manager Maria Kliavkoff.

Lurker was first produced on September 28, 1979 at Maclean Theatre in Iowa City, Iowa, and featured Chris Jansen as Lil and Don Nigro as Marston. It was directed by Sue Hickerson.

Lurker

(*LIL and MARSTON sitting in what may be a garden, suggested however only by the sound of birds at the beginning. MARSTON wears a rumpled suit. LIL wears an open shirt over a bikini. They speak at first neither to the audience nor to each other, exactly. The impression should be of something like interior monologue, but of interior monologue in which the other person is also imagined or in effect present.*)

MARSTON. I like to walk at night. I find it relaxing. At college I would walk in endless circles round the Oval, hearing sometimes the lovers in the dark, on the grass, under the trees. I was of course a different person then, in a different place. But I still walk. One night not long ago I was walking down a quiet residential street. A mosquito bit the back of my hand, I slapped at it and looked at my watch, it was just midnight, I heard the bell from the Church of Saint Francis on South Fifth Street, I turned to start for home and in doing so happened to look up at the second floor window of a house across the way and saw there the silhouette of a young woman removing her clothes.

LIL. Shame on you.

MARSTON. I stopped. I watched. After a moment the light went out. I was having some trouble swallowing, I think. An old man was walking his Pekinese past, and looking rather oddly at me. I walked on.

LIL. Let us understand, first of all, my priorities. I love my cat. I love my garden. I keep to myself. Each night at midnight I undress, and wash myself, and go to bed.

MARSTON. I was driving to work in the morning. The house was not exactly on my way, but it wasn't all that far

OUT of my way. I drove by. I stopped at a stop sign, and happened to glance towards the house. She had just come out the front door, dressed in a simple light bathrobe, to let the cat in, get the newspaper, check the mail box. I watched her bending down to pet the cat.

LIL. Nice kitty.

MARSTON. I would have driven on then, but the robe, you see, had come partly open for a moment. I could see very little, really, just some sort of nightgown and the hint of flesh beneath. Then she was gone into the house and the door was closed and I was still staring. I became aware that the car behind me was honking. I stepped on the gas and nearly hit a schoolbus broadside. The faces of the children in the windows, looking at me. I was nervous and upset for the rest of the day.

LIL. I paint, I take classes at the university on certain subjects which interest me, I have a small group of close friends. I keep to myself. I've learned that's the best way to keep one's — integrity — safe.

MARSTON. At night I took the same walk down the same street, I stopped across from the house, rather afraid I would meet the man with the Pekinese. Around midnight she appeared once again in the window undressing in silhouette. I had begun to sweat. My heart was pounding. I stood and stared.

LIL. I'm obsessive, I think. I make little rituals. I find patterns in my life, I cling to these patterns. This comforts me. When I am frightened I cling to patterns.

MARSTON. Driving to work in the morning I stopped at the stop sign and looked at the front of the house. The newspaper was there, mail in the mailbox, the cat waiting patiently, but no girl. The car behind me began to make unhappy noises. I drove around the block. When I had come around again to the stop sign, the newspaper, the mail, and the cat were gone, the door was just closing. I was impossible to get along with all day.

LIL. I believe in rituals. They give my life order. I'm terrified of disorder. I love my house, my garden, my cat, I do things very carefully, I'm a careful person. There are many horrors lurking in the dark places of the world. My father taught me that.

MARSTON. I called in sick at work, and in the afternoon I walked to the house, saw the alley behind the house, walked into the alley. I was very nervous. But I couldn't stop. There was a high wooden fence around the back yard.

LIL. My father built that.

MARSTON. I found a small hole in the fence. I hesitated, looked around to make sure no one was watching, and, taking a deep breath, I looked through the hole.

LIL. And what did you see?

MARSTON. It was a garden. There was a garden, a labyrinth of vines and flowered things, it was summer, you could hear the bees, it was lovely, all the carefully jungled growing things in there, and at the center of it was the girl in a two piece swimsuit, sunbathing, on the grass by three rose bushes.

LIL. White roses, and red.

MARSTON. I watched her. I forgot about the alley, my job, my life. I longed to be in that garden, with her, safe. I watched her lean over to pet the cat, the way the skin of her back moved as she twisted to scratch the cat. My legs were weak. I was trembling. I heard a noise. I turned back to the alley, annoyed and startled, and there down the alley was a boy of perhaps fifteen, astraddle a bicycle, stopped in the middle of the alley, staring at me. I walked away as slowly as I could, not looking back.

LIL. I read a great deal. I keep the house immaculate. I

take long baths. I dream sometimes I will die in the bath like Seneca or Agamemnon, sinking gently down into warm red water, after the first shock of penetration, of violation, a kind of pleasant sense of well-being, womblike.

MARSTON. Her body in the window. Her body in the garden. Her body in the bath. Touch it. I see her fingers touch her skin, her fingers move along her skin, exploring. I need to touch her.

LIL. I prick my finger on the rosebush. A sphere of blood appears on the tip of my finger. I lick it off. The garden smells so sweet, the honeysuckle. I lie in the sun, my skin touches the outside, but inside it's all different, but no one can see, no one can touch this.

MARSTON. I need to touch her.

LIL. In the garden there is a praying mantis by the four-o'clocks, watching, motionless. Image of God in the eye of the mantis. Cold eye, horrible. It devours the helpless. I stretch my body in the sun and think of lovers. One must be so careful. I live alone. I have a cat. When the grass is freshly cut in the garden the smell intoxicates.

MARSTON. That night I come to the house a few minutes late and she is just switching the light off. I cross the street and look up at her window from the yard. I go to the front door. I hesitate. I turn the knob. The door is locked. I am terrified at what I've done. What if the door had opened? I am a stranger to myself. I run home in the night sweating.

LIL. Sometimes, in the garden, I feel someone watching me.

MARSTON. In the afternoon I am in the alley again, looking through the fence. She is in the garden, in shorts and a small halter top, weeding around the three rose bushes. She looks up in my direction.

LIL. Is someone watching me?

MARSTON. I move quickly away from the hole in the fence and then freeze, unable to move. When I look again she has gone back to her work, but the cat is staring directly at me. I find this very annoying. The cat continues to stare at me. It occurs to me that I will kill the cat.

LIL. In the morning I open the door and get the paper, check the mail, let the cat in, and I feel that someone's eyes are on me.

MARSTON. I watch from the bushes beside the house in the morning, a few feet away from her. I have looked in her mailbox to see if she gets letters from other men. I no longer go to work at all. She is just a few feet away, I can smell her perfume. I have tried to catch the cat, but the cat eludes me. I hate this cat. The cat gets close to her, sees her naked, watches her bathe. I will hang the cat from a tree.

LIL. In the afternoon I tend the roses in the garden, and then lie in the sun. I feel the eyes watching me. I tend my father's garden. I wait.

MARSTON. She unties the top of her suit, I catch a glimpse of her breasts, and I clutch the fence until my fingers ache. The cat watches. I will kill the cat soon, the cat knows about me.

LIL. Nice kitty.

MARSTON. At night I stand in the yard and watch, and the cat watches ME. I try the door. I try the windows. I see the cat, looking at me. I stalk it carefully. I dive for it. The cat jumps onto a windowsill and into the house. The window is open. There is one open window at the side of the house. I look into the living room.

LIL. My father took me into the garden and taught me lessons. He lived in rituals.

MARSTON. I am trembling, I taste acid in the back of

my mouth, I seem to be driven by something that is not entirely myself. I crawl in the window.

LIL. Terror is a part of life. The tender are undone. Love kills.

MARSTON. Above, I hear water running.

LIL. At night I take off my clothes and run a warm bath.

MARSTON. The house is dark downstairs, but there is light above. I look at the dark furniture around me and think of her touching it, think of her naked above me, and I see the cat run up the stairs. I look up the stairs.

LIL. Death is sweet and more or less inevitable. The tender flowers are spoiled, ritually. My father taught me this. I mustn't be afraid.

MARSTON. I start carefully up the stairs. My heart is pounding. I can only think of her.

LIL. My father left me many things.

MARSTON. I reach the top of the stairs. There is light from one room. I move down the hallway.

LIL. He left me a lovely garden.

MARSTON. I go into the bedroom. Her clothing is draped on chairs and on the bed. Water is running in the bathroom beyond. I hear the faucet being turned off. Dripping, and a splashing noise.

LIL. He left me a sense of ritual.

MARSTON. I am shaking violently. I can hardly walk. I move cautiously to the bathroom door, which is partly open.

LIL. He left me a fine strange cat, all black.

MARSTON. I can see the end of the tub through the half open door, see the dripping faucet, hear the splash of water. I move towards it, in a dream, as something inevitable, a kind of terrible ritual.

LIL. He left me a set of long sharp knives.

MARSTON. I go into the bathroom. The tub is full of water, but she is not there.

LIL. One knife I like especially.

MARSTON. I hear the cat behind me, behind the door, and I turn in time, just, to see the girl's face as with both hands she brings the long sharp knife down into my eyes. (*pause*)

LIL. At night I dig in the garden, by my three beautiful rose bushes.

MARSTON. And now, decaying softly here beneath the fine rich soil of the garden, I understand, I think, and I do not object.

LIL. I go out in the afternoon to sit in the sun. I undo the top of my suit. Through the hole in the fence the cat can see a boy of perhaps fifteen, on a bicycle, watching me. I lie by my four lovely rose bushes, all in a row, and wonder where I shall put the next one. This is truth. This is my ritual, and the cat sees the boy through the fence and purrs and purrs.

The Devil

CHARACTERS:

Bontemps, a peasant
Mother Bontemps, his mother
La Rapet, an old nurse

SETTING:

The cottage of Mother Bontemps.

Based in part on a story by Guy de Maupassant.

The Devil was first presented in September, 1977 at Maclean Theatre in Iowa City, Iowa, with the following cast:

BONTEMPS .... Tim Clark
MOTHER BONTEMPS .... Martha Yates
LA RAPET .... Ellen Dolan

It was directed by Howard Blanning.

The Devil

Scene 1

(A bed, a table with chairs, a rocking chair by the bed, a ticking clock. A cupboard, a broom, some pots and pans. Morning. The sounds of farm animals. Chickens, roosters, cows, pigs and birds. BONTEMPS sleeps on the floor, snoring. A different, higher pitched and pathetic snoring and difficult breathing from MOTHER BONTEMPS, who is in the bed. The ticking of the clock. A particularly loud rooster. BONTEMPS awakes, with a good deal of hacking and spitting.)

BONTEMPS. Shit. (*He gets up with difficulty and goes over to examine MOTHER BONTEMPS, who is for the moment silent.*) Hello, Mama. Are you still with us? (*She snores, then gags.*)

MOTHER BONTEMPS. Urk. Ukkkk.

BONTEMPS. Still with us. Poor mama. How do you feel? Hey. Mama. How do you feel?

MOTHER BONTEMPS. (*stirring, croaking horribly, extremely weak, as if practicing a death rattle*) Urrrrrrk. Ukkkkkkkkkkkk.

BONTEMPS. Oh, better, huh?

MOTHER BONTEMPS. Arg.

BONTEMPS. That's my girl. Live until Christmas. See if I care. (*He opens his fly and goes out the door. Sound of a stream of water hitting the dirt. This goes on a bit.*)

LA RAPET. (*from off:*) Disgusting. Can't you go round back and do that?

BONTEMPS. And good morning to you, nursie, too.

LA RAPET. (*Entering*) Pig.

BONTEMPS. (*following her in*) Yes, I am fine, how are you?

LA RAPET. And your chickens are a disgrace.

BONTEMPS. I gave the best one to the doctor, may he rot in hell with my father.

LA RAPET. A man should watch out for his chickens. Chickens are God's birds.

BONTEMPS. (*making breakfast*) I told him the wheat's got to come in. It's too long on the ground already, I said, and the weather's ripe. When the wheat's ready, I said, what can I do? Is God going to wait on my mother to die, I said, or is he going to go ahead and rot the wheat?

LA RAPET. Talk nice about God. God watches. God does what he feels like. What's the matter with your mother?

BONTEMPS. She's going to turn up her toes and croak, that's what's the matter with her. Hello, mama. Are you dead?

LA RAPET. Is it as bad as all that?

BONTEMPS. He says she's lucky to last until morning. He called me a monster for wanting to get the wheat in. He won't allow it, he says. He says if I must get my wheat in, go fetch Rapet's wife to sit with my mother.

LA RAPET. Poor woman. She was always a good person. She went to church. She gave us apple jelly.

BONTEMPS. He said if I didn't pay someone to sit with her, he'd let me die like a dog when my turn comes. What kind of talk is that from a doctor?

LA RAPET. Poor Mother Bontemps. Your dancing days are done, aren't they? No more songs for you. The cow goes into the barn and doesn't come out again. No more pulling on Bossy's tits.

BONTEMPS. You know I'm not a rich man. How much will you charge me to sit with her so I can get the wheat

THE DEVIL

in? I can't afford much. We live in poverty here. I've been sick. I support my sister's children.

LA RAPET. You are a Christian martyr. There are two prices. Forty sous a day for the rich, and twenty a day for normal people. You can pay nineteen.

BONTEMPS. That's awfully high, nineteen a day. If I wasn't a sick man, perhaps, but—

LA RAPET. No bargains. You pay nineteen sous a day, or she can turn up her toes and croak all by herself. Excuse me, Mother Bontemps, but death is one thing and business is another.

BONTEMPS. Look, I'm a simple man. Adding up nineteens confuses me. Why don't we just settle on one sum, and you stay with her until she dies. The doctor says she'll go very soon. If she goes quickly, then it's a bargain for you. If she holds on a few more days, it's a bargain for me. We make it simple on ourselves and leave it in the hands of God. Is that fair?

LA RAPET. One sum, and I nurse her as long as she holds out?

BONTEMPS. If you think it's fair.

LA RAPET. Usually I'm paid by the day. I need to look at her.

BONTEMPS. You've already looked at her.

LA RAPET. For this I need to look closer.

BONTEMPS. She's not moving. Maybe she's dead already.

LA RAPET. (*examining MOTHER BONTEMPS*) No, we're not dead yet, are we, mother? No, we're strong. The pulse is so so. Breathing so so. Mother Bontemps. Mother Bontemps. Can you hear me, dearie?

MOTHER BONTEMPS. (*very weakly*) Yess.

LA RAPET. How do you feel, darling? Speak to me, sweetheart.

MOTHER BONTEMPS. Yess.

LA RAPET. But how do you feel, mother?

MOTHER BONTEMPS. Good. I feel good.

LA RAPET. She feels good. Could you sing songs for us, Mother Bontemps? Could you dance?

MOTHER BONTEMPS. (*a pathetic, feeble laugh*) Good. I feel good.

LA RAPET. This woman feels good.

BONTEMPS. So what's the price?

LA RAPET. She may last a little while. You'll have to give me six francs, everything included.

BONTEMPS. Six francs? SIX FRANCS? You're out of your mind. She can't last for six francs. I give her five or six hours at the most.

LA RAPET. Oh, excuse me, Mr. Expert. You know all about these things, do you? Tell me, please, which one of us has spent her whole life sitting up with dead people? You? You never sat up in your life. You sleep like a hog. I sat up, just last week, ten whole days with Sophie Padagnau. Before that I was nearly a month with Eulalie Ratier. And you scream like a pig when I say your mother may live a few more hours? Have some respect, why don't you. Death is very mysterious.

BONTEMPS. It's not worth six francs.

LA RAPET. I refuse to argue about such things. Go play in the wheat, and let your poor sainted mother turn up her toes and croak. I'm going home. People stink. Nobody cares. Poor old thing.

BONTEMPS. Wait. Just a minute.

LA RAPET. Goodbye, Mother Bontemps. I hope you come back and haunt this pig of a son you have. All he cares about is money.

BONTEMPS. All right. Six francs, including everything, until the corpse is taken out.

LA RAPET. Six francs. All right.

BONTEMPS. But you've got to sit with her every day, as long as she holds on, or I pay you nothing.

LA RAPET. I hear you. Six francs. Agreed.

BONTEMPS. Agreed. All right. This is robbery. You're lucky I'm so tender hearted. Well, goodbye, mama. Have a nice day.

MOTHER BONTEMPS. Urk. Ukk.

BONTEMPS. La Rapet will be good to you. Bye bye. (*He goes out.*)

LA RAPET. May the devil shit in your face. Where's the rocker? (*She sits down in the rocker, pulling it close to the bed.*) Nice, Mother Bontemps. I'll just sit right by you in this nice softy rocker and knit my grandson some underwear, heh? (*She begins rocking back and forth, creaking of the chair. She knits.*) Poor Mother Bontemps. If I had a son like yours I'd die just to be rid of him. What a pig. Don't you worry, dear, I'll take good care of you. We'll sing songs and tell old stories and laugh at the cat and have a wonderful time, won't we? And when you're feeling better, you can get up and dance for us, wouldn't you like that, Mother Bontemps?

MOTHER BONTEMPS. (*a girlish and hideously fetching old laugh, very weak*) Hee hee hee.

LA RAPET. You devil. Nice house you have, mother. Nice pots and pans, nice warm quilt, nice broom, nice meat cleaver, nice, cozy little world. Aren't we happy, mother? Snug as a bug, snug as a couple of wise old bugs and six francs richer, too. Nobody knows but us what it's like to be old and safe in the morning. (*She rocks, knits. Singing, to herself.*)*

Hear the church bells
early in the morning,
birth day, dying day,

---

*For music see page 113.

hear them sing—
(*An idea. Concerned.*) Mother Bontemps, I've just thought of something. Have you received the last sacrament?

MOTHER BONTEMPS. What?

LA RAPET. Has the curate been here? Have you confessed?

MOTHER BONTEMPS. Oh, yes. Yes.

LA RAPET. Thank God. At least the pig thought of *that*. You can't be too careful where God is concerned. God pays attention to things. God sees everything. He is always watching us to make sure we don't step in the shit. You think nice thoughts about God, mother, for God is great, God is good, and very mysterious, and he loves us very much, even you and me. Possibly also your son although I doubt it. God is only human. (*She rocks, knits, sings.*)
God in heaven,
Jesus in the garden,
devil in the bell-tower,
ding dong ding.
(*pause*) Mother Bontemps, how do you feel? Do you feel worse?

MOTHER BONTEMPS. Good. I feel good.

LA RAPET. That's my sweetie. If I was you I'd feel good too. Wouldn't you rather be you than me? Wouldn't you rather be there in a nice warm bed than sitting here waiting for some old lady to die? Do you know what happens when you die? You go up to heaven, of course. And do you know what happens in heaven, mother? Jesus is there. And Jesus is very handsome, like the pictures in the church, and he wears only a little cloth, like in the pictures of the cross, and he is very strong, and he puts his arms around you, Mother Bontemps, and he gives you a big kiss, right on your mouth. God is love, Mother Bontemps. Won't it be nice to go to heaven and rest forever in the arms of Jesus? I wish I was there myself.

MOTHER BONTEMPS. Good. I feel good. Nice. Hee hee.

LA RAPET. You feel good. That's my girlie. Will you sing me a song when you get to heaven? Will you have a dance with Jesus for me? Maybe you'd like to get up right now and do me a little dance, would you?

MOTHER BONTEMPS. Hee hee hee.

LA RAPET. Wouldn't you like to get up and smell the weeds and milk the goat again? God loves you, Mother Bontemps. Everybody loves you. Jesus loves you. And he only wears just a little cloth.

MOTHER BONTEMPS. I. Feel. Good.

LA RAPET. (*rocking and singing*)
Help me to your wine he said
let me sing my song.
Life is very short he said,
death is very long.
(*The creak creak of the rocker. Fade to dark.*)

SCENE 2

(*Three mornings later. BONTEMPS is slurping porridge at the table. LA RAPET is asleep in the rocker, snoring. Some rooster and cow carrying on, as before.*)

BONTEMPS. (*in mid-slurp*) Hey. Good morning.

LA RAPET. (*waking, mid-snore*) What? Antoine? Who?

BONTEMPS. Good morning.

LA RAPET. Oh. Is your mother dead yet?

BONTEMPS. Not at all. In fact, I think she's a little better.

LA RAPET. Is she?

BONTEMPS. Yes. She is. (*He slurps periodically.*) Three days, it's been. I begin to think she might hold on like this for weeks. Maybe months. I made a good bargain after all, didn't I? I'm getting my wheat in, and my mother has good company, and my six francs may just last through the winter. Pretty good bargain, huh? (*slurp*) Well, I've got to get to work. Hold on, mama. We all love you. Good day, ladies. (*He goes out laughing. Pause.*)

LA RAPET. (*quietly*) You eat like a pig. (*pause*) Well, how are you this morning, Mother Bontemps? It's cold this morning. Good morning.

MOTHER BONTEMPS. Yes.

LA RAPET. (*banging pots and pans, making warm milk*) Your son is in a good mood this morning. He thinks he's a genius like Napoleon.

MOTHER BONTEMPS. Good. I feel good.

LA RAPET. I bet you do. So many nice pots and pans, Mother Bontemps. Which one to pour the milk in? Is your pig son going to get all these? (*She pours milk into a pan.*) Nice little world here. Me to wait on you. Pots and pans. Warm milk for mother. Wheat coming in. Genius son. Six francs. Mother Bontemps feels good, does she?

MOTHER BONTEMPS. Good. I feel—

LA RAPET. I could be earning lots of money somewhere else today, you know that, Mother Bontemps? People are dying left and right. Rich people who pay plenty by the day. Yes. And I have to sit here and look at your idiot son google at me over the six francs he is paying me to sit with you until maybe doomsday. God

THE DEVIL

pays back people like your son. God is very just. Wouldn't it be nice to go to heaven and see God, Mother Bontemps? Do you know what God is like?

MOTHER BONTEMPS. Yes. No.

LA RAPET. (*pouring milk into a cup*) God is like the priest, Mother Bontemps. When you get to heaven, he takes your money, and if you've been good, he sends you to Jesus for a big kiss. But people like your son he takes out to the shithouse and stuffs walnuts up their nose. Won't it be nice to go to heaven and watch God stuff walnuts up your son's nose? Yes?

MOTHER BONTEMPS. Hee hee.

LA RAPET. (*helping her drink the milk*) Hee hee, she says. Where is the look, Mother Bontemps? I've been waiting to see the look. That's my secret, you know. Don't spit up your milk, dear. That's how I know someone is going to die. I see the look. The face turns in, they look at me and don't look at me like they're going on a trip and I can't come. They are far away and they feel sorry for us living people and sad about us and they hate us just a little because they see that we are thinking more about our own living than about their dying. They see it, and they get the look, and they die. That's how it always is, Mother Bontemps. I thought I saw it. So why don't I see it now? Are you going backwards? Am I going to spend the whole winter here for a lousey six francs? Is that fair? Would God like that? Oh, well, it's in his hands. The look is there, I think. Yes, I see it now. No more songs for you, mother. Maybe today. Yes, I think it's today. (*She settles back and begins to rock. Singing:*)
Hear the church bells
ringing in the morning,
death day, wedding day,

hear them sing,
God in heaven,
Jesus in the garden,
　MOTHER BONTEMPS. (*Croaking rather loudly.*)
DING DONG DING.
DING DONG DING.

(*Pause. LA RAPET stops rocking and stares, open mouthed.*)

　LA RAPET. Singing. You're SINGING. You're supposed to be dying, not singing. What is that smile on your face? Did I imagine that? Mother Bontemps?
　MOTHER BONTEMPS. (*a random ding*) Ding.
　LA RAPET. (*Watching her intently, beginning to sing again, cautiously.*)

God in heaven,	MOTHER BONTEMPS:
Jesus in the garden,	(*Joining in to make an*
devil in the bell-tower	*eerie round.*)
ding dong ding.	God in heaven,
Hear the church bells	Jesus in the garden
Early in the morning	devil in the bell-tower
birth day, dying day—	DING DONG DING.

　LA RAPET. Mother Bontemps—
　MOTHER BONTEMPS. (*Continuing, oblivious, ecstatic.*)
DING DONG DING
DING DONG DING
DING DONG DING
DING DONG—
　LA RAPET. MOTHER BONTEMPS! MOTHER BONTEMPS! MOTHER BONTEMPS! (*Pause. Silence.*)
　MOTHER BONTEMPS. Hmmm?

LA RAPET. Are you sure the curate has been here? You've confessed? One can't be too careful, Mother Bontemps, when one is about to die. One could take too much time along the way and forget some sin or other and end up in hell with the devil. Do you know what hell is like, Mother Bontemps?

MOTHER BONTEMPS. I feel—

LA RAPET. Hell is a place where you have to sit around with dead people for the rest of your life and they never go away and there is nothing to do but pick your nose and fart. You got the curate, did you?

MOTHER BONTEMPS. I feel—

LA RAPET. I know. Like dying. It's coming. Isn't it coming? Yes, I can definitely see it around the eyes. Don't be afraid, Mother Bontemps. Shall I run and get the curate?

MOTHER BONTEMPS. He's been.

LA RAPET. He's been?

MOTHER BONTEMPS. He's been.

LA RAPET. Oh, well, that's all right, then, isn't it? (*LA RAPET rocks, very upset.*) It's going to be a long cold winter, Mother Bontemps. Heaven is warmer. Not warmer than hell, but better than here, don't you think? Why are you smiling like that? What's to smile about? (*Pause. She sings, uneasy.*)

Help me to your wine he said let me sing my song—

MOTHER BONTEMPS. (*finishing the verse, this time rather beautifully*)
Life is very short he said,
death is very long.
Death is very long.
Death is very long.
Death is very long.
Death is very—

LA RAPET. (*Enormously agitated.*) You really shouldn't sing, Mother Bontemps. It's not good for you. I think you should stop that. God will rot the chickens. No more sucking on bossy's tits.

MOTHER BONTEMPS. Hee hee hee. Hee hee.

LA RAPET. What's so funny?

MOTHER BONTEMPS. I feel —

LA RAPET. What? What? You feel like what?

MOTHER BONTEMPS. I feel — like — dancing.

LA RAPET. You feel like dancing?

MOTHER BONTEMPS. I feel like dancing. I feel like dancing. I feel like dancing. I feel like dancing. I feel like dancing. I feel like —

LA RAPET. MOTHER BONTEMPS. MOTHER BONTEMPS. BE QUIET, WILL YOU? (*Pause. LA RAPET tries to calm herself.*) Do you know what I think? I think the devil has come. I think the devil is making you act so strangely. You're not acting like a normal dying person. And somebody here must be dying. And it isn't me. I don't think it's me. Is it me? Of course it's not me. The devil is here. It's the devil.

MOTHER BONTEMPS. (*vaguely*) Ohhhhhhhh?

LA RAPET. Mother Bontemps, have you seen the devil yet? Have you? Have you seen the devil?

MOTHER BONTEMPS. Who?

LA RAPET. The devil. Didn't you know that, some minutes before one dies, the devil appears? Didn't you know that?

MOTHER BONTEMPS. The devil?

LA RAPET. You'd better close your eyes, Mother Bontemps, or you'll see the devil, and everything will be over. The person who sees the devil knows they have only a moment to live.

MOTHER BONTEMPS. The devil?

LA RAPET. Close your eyes, mother. I can smell him. He's around somewhere. Close your eyes or he'll get you.

MOTHER BONTEMPS. Yes, all right. (*She closes her eyes tight.*)

LA RAPET. Good. Close them tight, now. (*LA RAPET gets up, carefully, muttering to herself.*) Where is the quilt? There. Broom. There is the broom. (*Out loud, to MOTHER BONTEMPS.*) The devil appears just before you die, and he has a broom in his hand, and a cape of many colors, and a saucepan on his head — (*muttering*) — saucepan — there's one — (*aloud*) And he utters loud and horrible cries.

MOTHER BONTEMPS. Horrible cries?

LA RAPET. Yes, it's quite common. It's a terrible thing. Terrible. (*She wraps the quilt around her and puts the saucepan on her head.*)

MOTHER BONTEMPS. The devil?

LA RAPET. Oh, yes, and he makes such awful noises — (*She gets an old tin pan and a large wooden spoon.*) I've heard of it many times. Eulalie Ratier saw the devil before she died. (*She gets a washboard.*) And so did Josephine Loisel and Sophie Padagnau, and Seraphine Grospied. Keep your eyes closed.

MOTHER BONTEMPS. (*Very upset.*) Horrible cries?

LA RAPET. (*Pulling a chair over to the foot of the bed.*) Urf. Horrible. Just horrible.

MOTHER BONTEMPS. (*Trying to cheer herself up.*) Ding dong ding.
Dong ding ding.

(*LA RAPET climbs upon the chair, wrapped in the quilt, saucepan on her head, holding tin pan, washboard, and broom.*)

LA RAPET. Mother Bontemps, open your eyes and look.

MOTHER BONTEMPS. No. The devil.
LA RAPET. Open your eyes. It's all right.
MOTHER BONTEMPS. The devil. No.
LA RAPET. No, it's Jesus, Mother Bontemps, he's looking in at the window, it's Jesus, mother, Jesus has come to see you.
MOTHER BONTEMPS. No.
LA RAPET. Yes. And he only wears a little cloth.
MOTHER BONTEMPS. Does he?
LA RAPET. Yes. Look. He wants to kiss you. Look.
MOTHER BONTEMPS. Oh. All right. (*She opens her eyes.*) Jesus?
LA RAPET. (*immediately banging on the washboard and the tin pan, waving the broom, uttering the most horrible cries and screeches imaginable*) AAAAAAAAHHHHHHHH!!! OOOOOOOOOOOO!! EEEEEEEEEEEEE!! URRRRR!! RRRRRRRRRZZZZZZZZZ!! DDDDDDDDDDDDDD!!!
MOTHER BONTEMPS. (*screaming, terrified, echoing her*) AHHHHHHHHHHHH!! OOOOOOOOO!! EEEEEEEE!! AZZAAAA!
LA RAPET. (*banging away in a frenzy*) EKKKKKKK!! GRRRUNNNNNNZZZZZZ!! BLAAAHHHHHHHH!!
MOTHER BONTEMPS. (*choking and gagging*) erf. ukkk. igk. erup. (*She falls back onto the pillow and stops moving. Pause.*)
LA RAPET. (*whispering, very gentle*) Mother Bontemps? Are you dead? Mother? (*She gets down off the chair and goes to the bed, peering carefully at MOTHER BONTEMPS.*) Are you dead, dear?
MOTHER BONTEMPS. (*looking up, seeing the saucepanned head of LA RAPET, immediately*)

EEEEEEEEEEEKKKKK!!!!   OOOOOOOOOOHH-HH!! BLAAAHHHHHH!

La Rapet. (*horribly frightened by this, then rallying and resuming as before with more vigor*) EEEEEEEEEEEEE!!!   OOOOOOOOO!!!   Shit. WOOOOOOOOOOOOOOO!!   BLAAAAAAAAHH-HHHHHHH!!!!   BOOGELDY   BOOGELDY!! OOOOOOO!! GRRRRRRRRR!!! URRRFFFFFF.

Mother Bontemps. AHHHHHH!! AHHHHHH!! AHHH — urk — ufl — gikk. (*horrible gasping and choking sounds*) — iggggggg. (*She lies motionless. Pause.*)

La Rapet. (*just to make sure*) Now? One for Jesus? BLAAAAAAAAAAAAAAHHH!! (*A few more stray beats on the tin pan.*) Poor Mother Bontemps. You're dead. (*She begins carefully putting away the pans, the washboard, the broom, the spoon, the quilt, talking as she goes.*) Poor baby. God has taken her. Oh, we'll close your sweet eyes — (*She closes her eyes.*) — and we'll pray a bit and call the curate. Poor mother. (*singing, sadly:*)
Help me to your wine he said,
let me sing my song.
Life is very short he said,
death is very long.

(*She kneels down by the bed to pray.*)

Bible

CHARACTERS:

Mama, a beautiful young woman dressed handsomely in neo-Victorian finery

Annabel, her beautiful daughter, actually a petite adult actress dressed as a little girl

Harry, Mama's handsome son, actually a smallish adult actor dressed as a little boy

SETTING: A park bench.

Bible

(*MAMA is out for a stroll with her lovely children ANNA-BEL and HARRY. They are passing a park bench. ANNABEL carries a Bible.*)

MAMA. Oh, children, these summer rambles in the park are such fun, do you not think so, dears?

ANNABEL. Yes, Mama.

HARRY. Yes, Mama.

ANNABEL. Pray, Mama, tell us, where is our Papa today?

MAMA. Papa is at work, Annabel, of course, as he always is.

ANNABEL. And what does Papa do, Mama, at work? Pray, tell us again.

MAMA. Papa is—hands out of pockets, Harry, naughty boy—Papa is a Christian censor, dear.

ANNABEL. And what does a Christian censor do, Mama?

MAMA. He burns books, dear, and puts terrible writers in jail, where they belong, and he destroys all pictures of persons in a state of undress.

ANNABEL. But, Mama, if Daddy burns books, then why do we have this book?

MAMA. Because that book, Annabel, is the Bible, and is an Holy Book. Daddy does not burn books like that, dear, he only burns the bad books, with pictures of unclothed persons in them, or descriptions of body functions, or other such unnatural things.

HARRY. What is a body function, Mama?

MAMA. Nothing you should be concerned about, Harry. You are just a little boy.

ANNABEL. Would you read to us from this book, Mama?

MAMA. Read to you?

ANNABEL. Yes, Mama. We do so wish you to read to us from this book, don't we, Harry?

HARRY. No. It's a book, Mama. There might be body functions in it, that would jump out and hurt us.

MAMA. Nonsense, Harry. This is a wonderful book. The Bible is an Holy book. Always remember that. Why, you can just open this book anywhere, anywhere at all, and come upon some wondrous, inspiring story, and always very clean, for there is nothing a bit unclean in the Bible, it is God's book.

ANNABEL. Oh, then, do read us something, Mama, for we are ever so interested in books that are clean and wholesome.

MAMA. Well, but children, there are so many wonderful things in the Bible, I don't know which story to pick.

ANNABEL. Just open it at random, Mama, then, and God will pick us a story to read today.

MAMA. Well—

ANNABEL. Oh, please, Mama, please? Oh, please?

MAMA. All right. That might be morally instructive and profitable for us, children, to let God choose us a wonderful and inspiring story to read, from his Holy book. I will just open the book at random, letting the Holy Spirit direct my fingers, and show you what glorious treasures are lurking in this Holy book.

ANNABEL. Oh, isn't this exciting, Harry?

HARRY. No.

MAMA. (*opening the Bible, closing her eyes, sticking her finger on a passage, then opening her eyes*) God has chosen for us Genesis, chapter thirty-eight. (*She begins to read.*)

BIBLE

And it came to pass at that time
that Judah went down from his brethren
and turned in to a certain Adullamite,
whose name was Hirah.

HARRY. This is boring, Mama.

ANNABEL. Shush, Harry, it's supposed to be boring, it's religious.

MAMA. Religion is not boring, Annabel. God just makes it appear that way at first glance in order to test our sincerity. Now, pay attention so that you may be properly edified.

ANNABEL. Yes, Mama.

MAMA. (*reading*)
And Judah saw there a daughter
of a certain Canaanite whose name
was Shuah, and he took her,
and went unto her.

HARRY. What does that mean, Mama?

MAMA. Well, it means that, um, probably he took her by the hand, and they went into her tent. To play.

HARRY. Were they camping, Mama?

MAMA. Well, yes, Harry, in those days, everybody camped out in the desert. It was a very long time ago. Would you rather we did something else, dear?

ANNABEL. No, Mama, do please go on, it is so edifying, hearing God's word.

MAMA. As you wish. (*reading*)
And she conceived, and bare a son,
and she called his name Er.

ANNABEL. What is 'conceived,' Mama?

MAMA. She had a baby, dear, a little baby boy, and they called him Er.

HARRY. That's a funny name, Mama.

MAMA. Yes, they all had funny names then, Harry, for

it was near the beginning of the world, and they had not yet had time to discover beautiful names like Harry and Annabel.

ANNABEL. Why did she conceive, Mama?

MAMA. Because God wanted her to. It was all part of his plan.

HARRY. And who was the baby's Papa, Mama?

MAMA. It must have been Judah, dear.

HARRY. Is that what they were doing in the tent? Conceiving?

MAMA. It must be, although it does not actually say, that they got married in the tent, so that the Canaanite's daughter could conceive. Maybe you'd like to go and play now with the neighbor's dog, Bowser.

HARRY. Oh, no, Mama, Bowser is very large, and frightens me so, and slobbers upon my face, and clutches onto my leg. Read us some more Bible, it is not so boring as I had thought at first.

ANNABEL. Yes, Mama, do.

MAMA. All right. (*reading*) And she conceived again, and bare a son, and she called his name Onan.

HARRY. Another funny name, Mama. Is no one in the Bible named Edward, or Percy, or Basil, or other good names?

MAMA. I don't know, dear. Perhaps in the New Testament.

ANNABEL. Read more, Mama.

HARRY. Yes, do.

MAMA. (*reading, but getting rather uncomfortable*)
And she yet again conceived,
and bare a son,
and called his name Shelah,
and he was at Chezib
when she bare him.

HARRY. Shelah? A little boy named Shelah?

ANNABEL. I know a girl named Shelah.

MAMA. Yes, well, this was a little BOY named Shelah.

HARRY. Did they have then little boys named Gertrude, and Priscilla, and Prudence, in the Bible, also?

MAMA. I don't think so, dear.

ANNABEL. Why did they do so much conceiving, Mama?

MAMA. Because, dear, it was so near the beginning of the world, that God needed more people.

HARRY. They must have spent a great deal of time in their tents, Mama, if they were conceiving so much.

MAMA. Yes, dear, well, probably also it was very hot outside, in fact, I'm getting a little warm myself. Perhaps we should go inside and take our nap, now, would you like that?

ANNABEL. Oh, no, Mama, I want to hear more about the conceiving.

HARRY. Please, Mama.

ANNABEL. Please? Please?

MAMA. (*smiling grimly and reading*) And Judah took a wife for Er, his firstborn,
whose name was Tamar.

HARRY. Oh, Er has grown up so quickly, Mama.

MAMA. Yes, Harry, that's because he ate all his vegetables, and was a good boy.

HARRY. Oh, Mama, does this mean that if I eat all my vegetables, I can grow up as quickly as Er did, and begin conceiving?

MAMA. Only women can conceive, dear. Let's continue. (*reading*) And Er, Judah's firstborn, was wicked in the sight of the Lord, and the Lord slew him.

ANNABEL. Oh, poor Er. He has just barely been conceived, and now already the Lord has slewn him.

HARRY. Why did the Lord slew Er, Mama?

MAMA. Because he was wicked, dear.

HARRY. But you just said that Er was a good boy, and ate all his vegetables.

MAMA. Well, he must have stopped eating his vegetables, and that's why God slew him.

ANNABEL. Why does God feel so deeply about vegetables, Mama?

MAMA. Because the vegetables are his children, also, dear. Now, I really think that's quite enough Bible reading for today —

ANNABEL. Oh, no, Mama, please, I want to find out if the other little boys, Onan and Shelah, are also slewn.

HARRY. Yes, Mama, yes, yes.

MAMA. All right, but Mama needs a drink of her medicine first. (*She takes out a little bottle and drinks.*) There. Mama feels better. Now. Where are we? Here. (*reading*) And Judah said unto Onan, Go in unto thy brother's wife, and marry her, and raise up seed to thy brother.

HARRY. Why did Judah want Onan to marry his brother's wife, Mama?

ANNABEL. To raise up seed to his brother, Harry. You must try and pay better attention to God's word.

HARRY. I AM paying attention, Annabel, do not scold me. I simply do not understand what seed has got to do with it. Cannot he plant seed without marrying his brother's wife? What a funny thing.

MAMA. The Bible is never funny, Harry. Judah must have felt sad for poor Tamar, who was no doubt very lonely after the Lord slew her husband Er, and so Judah gave to Tamar his other son, Onan, to comfort her, and he must have helped her with the farming.

HARRY. And then what happened, Mama?

BIBLE

MAMA. Well, it says — (*reading*) And Onan knew that the seed should not be his, and it came to pass, when he went in unto his brother's wife, that he spilled it on the ground, lest that he should give seed to his brother.

HARRY. What did he spill on the ground, Mama?

MAMA. The seed, dear.

HARRY. But why, Mama?

MAMA. Lest that he should give seed to his brother.

HARRY. But his brother was dead, remember? The Lord slew him. And Onan has just married Tamar, his brother's wife, and then he has gone in unto her, and spilled his seed on the ground. Onan is very sloppy with his seed, is he not? I don't understand this at all.

MAMA. This is just something that married people do, dear.

HARRY. You and Papa are married, does Papa ever come unto you and spill his seed on the ground?

MAMA. No, dear, not usually, but I am not your father's brother's widow — if so, I would not be your Mama, I would be your Auntie, and also, we are not farmers, and, in any case, it must have been a very wicked thing for Onan to have done, for in the next verse it says — (*reading*) And the thing which he did displeased the Lord, wherefore he slew him also.

ANNABEL. Oh, no, the Lord has slewn Onan, also?

MAMA. That's what it says.

ANNABEL. But for what, Mama?

MAMA. For spilling his seed upon the ground.

HARRY. Oh, Mama, I don't ever wish to be a farmer, for I might accidentally spill my seed upon the ground, and then the Lord would slew me also, as he did poor Er and Onan.

ANNABEL. The Lord seems very cross in this chapter, does he not, Mama?

MAMA. It is not for us to judge the Lord, Annabel. We must simply do his bidding. Now, I definitely think we've had quite enough of this—

ANNABEL. Oh NO.

HARRY. No, Mama, please.

ANNABEL. We can't stop yet, please, oh please.

HARRY. Don't stop, Mama, don't stop, don't stop.

ANNABEL. We wish to know what happens to poor little Shelah, who is the only brother left.

MAMA. But Mama is tired, children.

HARRY. Have some more medicine, then, Mama. That always makes you feel better.

MAMA. This is true. Perhaps I will. (*She takes another swig of medicine.*)

ANNABEL. Feel better, Mama?

MAMA. You bet. Okay. (*She reads.*) Then said Judah to Tamar, his daughter in law, Remain a widow at thy father's house, till Shelah my son be grown: for he said, Lest peradventure he die also, as his brethren did. And Tamar went and dwelt in her father's house.

HARRY. Oh, poor Shelah. He had better not go and marry his brother's wife again, or the Lord will slew him.

ANNABEL. Only if he spills his seed.

HARRY. Er did not spill his seed, and the Lord slew Er.

ANNABEL. We don't know whether Er spilled his seed or not.

HARRY. It doesn't say that Er spilled his seed. It just says the Lord slew him, is that not right, Mama?

MAMA. Children, children, do not quarrel, we must not fight over the word of God. We must leave that to persons more religious than ourselves.

HARRY. Will the Lord then be displeased with us, if we fight over his word, and slew us?

ANNABEL. Only if we spill our seed.

HARRY. I haven't got any seed.

MAMA. If you children are going to be foul and unChristian with one another, Mama is not going to finish reading the story.

ANNABEL. Oh, no, Mama, we'll be ever so good, we promise, don't we, Harry?

HARRY. Yes, Mama, we'll be good, please go on, have some more medicine.

MAMA. All righty. (*She takes another drink of medicine.*) Well, then, let's just finish this little fishy all up, shall we? (*reading*) And in the process of time, the daughter of Shuah, Judah's wife, died; and Judah was comforted, and went up unto his sheepshearers to Timnath, he and his friend Hirah the Adullamite.

ANNABEL. Why did it comfort Judah, that his wife had died?

HARRY. Probably she was cross and ugly, like Annabel.

MAMA. Harry.

ANNABEL. Harry, you are a dirty, ill-smelling snotbooger.

MAMA. Annabel, your brother is not a snotbooger.

ANNABEL. Have some more medicine, Mama.

MAMA. All right. (*She drinks some more medicine.*)

ANNABEL. Snotbooger.

HARRY. Mama, Annabel called me a snotbooger again.

MAMA. There will be no more snotboogering in my presence, is that clear?

ANNABEL. Yes, Mama.

HARRY. Yes, Mama.

ANNABEL. But Harry said I was cross and ugly.

HARRY. It was only an example, to demonstrate why Judah may have been comforted by his wife dying.

MAMA. Children, you have misconstrued.

ANNABEL. I never did, Mama, I swear.

MAMA. No, Judah was not comforted because his wife had died. He was comforted by his sheepshearers. I imagine that being up there among the sheep made him feel better. Sheep are very soft and comforting. Now, apologize to your sister, Harry, for saying that she is cross and ugly.

HARRY. I am sorry, Annabel, that you are cross and ugly.

MAMA. Harry. Don't be a snotbooger.

HARRY. I am sorry I said that you are cross and ugly, Annabel.

ANNABEL. And I forgive you for it, Harry, because that is what Jesus would do, and, besides, you will burn in hell for your sins.

MAMA. That is so good of you, Harry and Annabel. And now, Harry, kiss your sister, and make up.

HARRY. I don't want to kiss my sister, Mama, lest the Lord be displeased and slew me.

MAMA. The Lord will not slew you for kissing your sister, Harry. Go on.

ANNABEL. You may kiss me, Harry, if you wish.

HARRY. All right. But I want the Lord to observe that I am not spilling any seed upon the ground.

MAMA. He will see that, Harry, the Lord sees everything, we do not need to draw attention to what we do.

HARRY. Then I will kiss my sister. (*He kisses ANNABEL on the cheek.*) There. I have kissed my sister, Lord, without spilling any seed upon the ground.

MAMA. There. That was not so bad, was it, Harry?

HARRY. No, Mama, it was rather nice, actually. And to show that there are no hard feelings, I will kiss my sister once again. (*He kisses her on the lips.*) There. I have kissed my sister on the lips, to show that I do as Jesus would do. And it was not bad at all. And furthermore, Jesus is welcome to kiss my sister, any time he wishes. I think I shall kiss my sister once more. (*He takes ANNABEL into his arms and gives her a passionate, desperate soul kiss.*)

MAMA. (*drinking*) My, what a good little boy you are. This medicine is certainly making me feel wonderfully better. Harry, that's fine. Harry? Harry, this is quite enough sister-kissing for one day. Harry. Harry, you will spill your seed.

HARRY. (*Coming up for air.*) I like being a good Christian, Mama.

MAMA. Yes, Harry, but we mustn't overdo it, must we? (*She pulls him away from the now prone ANNABEL by grabbing the hair at the top of his head with her fist.*)

HARRY. YAAAAAAAAAAAAAAAA. That hurts, Mama.

MAMA. That's nice, dear.

ANNABEL. (*lying on the ground, legs spread apart, panting*) Harry can kiss me again, Mama, if he wants to.

MAMA. Get up, Annabel, we're going to finish the story.

HARRY. I'll help her up, Mama.

MAMA. You stay here. (*She grabs his hair again and pulls him back.*)

HARRY. YAAAAAAAAAAAAAAA.

MAMA. (*reading*) And it was told Tamar, saying, Behold, thy father in law goeth up to Timnath to shear his sheep. And she put her widow's garments off from her, and covered her with a veil, and wrapped herself, and sat in an open place, which is by the way to Timnath; for she saw that Shelah was grown, and she was not given him to wife. When Judah saw her, he thought her to be an harlot, because she had covered her face. (*closing the book*) And so they all lived happily ever after. The end.

ANNABEL. What is an harlot, Mama?

MAMA. An harlot is a very bad woman, Annabel, and this is not something that children should be speaking of.

ANNABEL. But it's in the Bible, Mama. You said that everything in the Bible is clean and wholesome.

MAMA. And so it is, dear.

ANNABEL. Then why cannot you read to us about an harlot?

HARRY. Is the Bible a bad book, then, Mama?

MAMA. Certainly not. The Bible is the most wonderful book in the whole world.

ANNABEL. Then read to us the rest of the story, please, Mama, as I, for one, wish to be edified more deeply yet.

MAMA. (*smiling cooly, opening the book again, and reading*) And he turned unto her by the way, and said, Go to, I pray thee, let me come in unto thee — (*reading ahead silently*) Oh, dear.

ANNABEL. You must read out loud, Mama, if Harry and I are to continue to be edified.

MAMA. Oh, all right, all right, keep your knickers on, Annabel.

ANNABEL. Mama.

MAMA. It's all right, dear. That is a Biblical expression, used, I believe, by Joseph when speaking to Potiphar's wife. Now. Where was we? Excuse me. (*She takes another drink.*)

HARRY. Oh, pray, do not waste so much time in drinking your medicine, Mama, and get on with the story, we wish to know what happens with Judah and the harlot.

MAMA. Oh, jabber jabber jabber. Here, have some medicine, it will pacify you somewhat.

HARRY. I don't want any medicine, Mama.
MAMA. Take it.
HARRY. No.
MAMA. Take it, Harry, or I'll cut off your little pee pee.
HARRY. (*alarmed*) All right, Mama, I'll drink it, I'll drink it. (*He takes the bottle and drinks.*)
ANNABEL. Mama, is not Harry too young to be drinking your medicine?
MAMA. You're never too young to take your medicine, Annabel, remember that. You have some, too, it'll edify you.
ANNABEL. All right, Mama, if you say so, only please continue.
HARRY. Ummmm, this is good medicine, Mama.
MAMA. Drink it, Annabel, it'll put hair on your wee wee.
ANNABEL. Mama, I don't think we ought to be talking about my wee wee in front of Harry.
MAMA. If we can talk about Harry's little pee pee, we can certainly talk about the hair on your wee wee.
ANNABEL. But Mama, what would Papa say?
MAMA. Oh, poop on Papa, he's got a smaller pee pee than Harry does.
ANNABEL. (*drinking*) You're right, Harry. This IS good medicine.
MAMA. So. Where was I about to continue when I was so rudely forced to abridge my expostulation? Oh, here —(*She looks at the book, puzzled.*) What is this? Hebrew?
ANNABEL. You have the book upside down, Mama.
MAMA. The Bible makes the same sense when read in any direction whatsoever, Annabel. That's the beauty of it. However, since you are only children, I shall read it in the conventional way for the present. (*She turns the book*

right side up.) Now—(*She reads.*) Let me come in unto thee—for he knew not that she was his daughter in law—And she said, What wilt thou give me, that thou mayest come in unto me?

ANNABEL. (*passing the medicine back and forth with HARRY and MAMA*) I don't understand, Mama. Is Tamar charging Judah to come into her tent?

MAMA. Well, it's sort of a tent. It's a wee wee little tent. (*She giggles at her joke.*) Hee heehee hee heeeee.

ANNABEL. But why, Mama?

MAMA. This is something harlots do, it's sort of a user's fee, as when Papa goes on the turnpike. (*reading*) And he said, I will send thee a kid from the flock. A kid, you must understand, children, is a small goat. You see, Judah is an honorable man, he is giving his daughter in law a goat.

HARRY. But Papa does not pay with a goat when he goes on the turnpike.

MAMA. No, dear, a goat is just one form of exchange. He might just as easily have given her a goose. Your Papa often gives me a goose before he comes in unto me.

ANNABEL. But, Mama, why has Papa never given ME a goose?

MAMA. Perhaps some day he will, dear.

ANNABEL. Oh, I hope so. I should like so much to have a little goose.

MAMA. Now, Tamar, you see, furthermore, is a very smart girl, she sees that Judah does not happen to have brought a goat with him, and so she says—Wilt thou give me a pledge, till thou send it?—meaning, of course, the goat. —And he said, What pledge shall I give thee? And she said, Thy signet, and thy bracelets, and thy staff that is in thine hand.

HARRY. Why is Judah wearing bracelets, Mama? That is not a very manly thing, is it? Do you think his son Shelah also wears bracelets? And why does he have his staff in his hand?

MAMA. To keep it ready for emergencies, dear, or perhaps to use on the goat.

ANNABEL. This medicine is delightful.

MAMA. Don't hog all the medicine, Annabel.

HARRY. Read, Mama, read.

MAMA. (*reading*) And he gave it to her.

ANNABEL. (*getting woozy from the medicine*) What did she say?

HARRY. Judah is giving it to the harlot.

MAMA. (*reading*) —and he came in unto her—

ANNABEL. Pardon?

HARRY. Judah's coming in unto her.

MAMA. (*reading*) —and she conceived by him.

ANNABEL. There they go, conceiving again. And she being an harlot, and he being the father of her two dead husbands, and of poor Shelah as well? Oh, Mama, somebody is going to get slewn again, I just know it.

MAMA. Let us skip a bit here, children, so that we may finish before your father gets home from the book-burning furnaces.

ANNABEL. But what happens, Mama? Is somebody slewn?

MAMA. Judah sends her the goat, but they can't find the harlot anywhere, and naturally they're very perplexed—

ANNABEL. But was somebody slewn? Was they all slewn?

MAMA. I'm coming to it, I'm coming to it, don't wet your bloomers. (*reading*) And it came to pass about three months after, that it was told to Judah, saying, Tamar thy daughter in law hath played the harlot; and also, behold, she is with child, by whoredom.

HARRY. What is whoredom, Mama?

MAMA. Whoredom is harlotry in its vulgar form, Harry, and is a very evil thing. Tamar must be punished for this.

ANNABEL. I knew it. She's about to be slewn.

MAMA. (*reading*) And Judah said, Bring her forth, and let her be burnt.

HARRY. Judah is burning Tamar for being an harlot, Mama?

MAMA. Of course, Harry. She has allowed men not her husband to come in unto her and conceive with her.

ANNABEL. But, Mama, it was Judah who came in unto her. Why does not Judah burn also himself?

MAMA. Because Judah is a man, dear, and men do not burn themselves, they only burn women.

HARRY. And books, as Papa does.

MAMA. Yes, and books.

ANNABEL. Mama, that is not fair. That is not fair at all. If what Tamar has done is wrong, then what Judah has done is wrong also, is that not so?

MAMA. Annabel, we must never expect God to make sense. He has much more important things to worry about.

ANNABEL. But Mama—

MAMA. Oh, shut up, you ask too many damn questions, how the hell should I know? Judas Priest. Give me that medicine. (*She takes the medicine and drinks. ANNABEL is sad and thoughtful. Pause.*)

ANNABEL. Mama, can Harry kiss me again?

MAMA. No.

ANNABEL. Can he kiss me again if I let him call me cross and ugly first?

MAMA. No, there's not time, children, your Papa will be home soon.

ANNABEL. Oh, good, Mama, perhaps if I am a good girl, Papa will give me a goose.

HARRY. I want a goose, too.

ANNABEL. No, me.

HARRY. Me. MEEEEEE.

MAMA. Don't fight, children. We must all be innocent and pure, as in the Garden of Eden, when God's children were pure and innocent in their simple nakedness. And they were not ashamed.

ANNABEL. Were they quite naked in the Garden of Eden, Mama?

MAMA. Yes they were. As naked as slugs.

ANNABEL. Oh, Mama, I will be good, I will be pure and innocent so God will not slew me or burn me, I will remove all my clothing and surprise Papa when he gets home, and then perhaps he will give me a goose. (*She runs off excitedly.*)

MAMA. No, Annabel, wait, Annabel—Good Lord. Come on, Harry, come home with Mama.

HARRY. (*looking at the Bible*) Mama, if Papa burns books, then why has he not burned this book?

MAMA. Because, Harry, your father is a good Christian man, he only burns books with sex and violence in them. Now, come along, let us go home so we can greet your Papa at the door, and perhaps he will give you a goose, as well. Come on.

ANNABEL. (*from off, shouting:*) Look, Mama. Look at me. I am naked. I am naked.

MAMA. Yes, Annabel, that's very nice.

ANNABEL. And I am not ashamed.

MAMA. We can see that, dear.

HARRY. (*looking at ANNABEL*) Oh, Mama. I must run and apologize to Annabel again. I will be naked and not ashamed with her.

MAMA. Just a minute. Harry— (*HARRY runs off.*) Harry. (*She looks after him.*) Ah, well. (*She picks up the Bible he has left. It falls open. She looks at the passage that is revealed, reading:*) Let him kiss me with the kisses of his mouth, for thy love is better than wine. (*pause*) What a genuinely wise and beautiful book this is. Wait, children. Allow me to disrobe with you. What a surprise for Papa. We shall all greet him in a state of naked unashamedness. Papa will be so surprised. He will be so surprised.

(*She runs off after them, distractedly leaving the Bible on the bench. Lights fade on it. Darkness.*)

Other Publications for Your Interest

THE CURATE SHAKESPEARE AS YOU LIKE IT
(LITTLE THEATRE—COMEDY)

By DON NIGRO

4 men, 3 women—Bare stage

This extremely unusual and original piece is subtitled: "The record of one company's attempt to perform the play by William Shakespeare". When the very prolific Mr. Nigro was asked by a professional theatre company to adapt *As You Like It* so that it could be performed by a company of seven he, of course, came up with a completely original play about a rag-tag group of players comprised of only seven actors led by a dotty old curate who nonetheless must present Shakespeare's play; and the dramatic interest, as well as the comedy, is in their hilarious attempts to impersonate all of Shakespeare's multitude of characters. The play has had numerous productions nationwide, all of which have come about through word of mouth. We are very pleased to make this "underground comic classic" widely available to theatre groups who like their comedy wide open and theatrical. (#5742)

(Royalty, $50-$25.)

SEASCAPE WITH SHARKS AND DANCER
(LITTLE THEATRE—DRAMA)

By DON NIGRO

1 man, 1 woman—Interior

This is a fine new play by an author of great talent and promise. We are very glad to be introducing Mr. Nigro's work to a wide audience with *Seascape With Sharks and Dancer*, which comes directly from a sold-out, critically acclaimed production at the world-famous Oregon Shakespeare Festival. The play is set in a beach bungalow. The young man who lives there has pulled a lost young woman from the ocean. Soon, she finds herself trapped in his life and torn between her need to come to rest somewhere and her certainty that all human relationships turn eventually into nightmares. The struggle between his tolerant and gently ironic approach to life and her strategy of suspicion and attack becomes a kind of war about love and creation which neither can afford to lose. In other words, this is quite an offbeat, wonderful love story We would like to point out that the play also contains a wealth of excellent **monologue** and **scene material.** (#21060)

(Royalty, $50-$35.)

Other Publications for Your Interest

SEASCAPE WITH SHARKS AND DANCER
(LITTLE THEATRE—DRAMA)

By DON NIGRO

1 man, 1 woman—Interior

This is a fine new play by an author of great talent and promise. We are very glad to be introducing Mr. Nigro's work to a wide audience with *Seascape With Sharks and Dancer*, which comes directly from a sold-out, critically acclaimed production at the world-famous Oregon Shakespeare Festival. The play is set in a beach bungalow. The young man who lives there has pulled a lost young woman from the ocean. Soon, she finds herself trapped in his life and torn between her need to come to rest somewhere and her certainty that all human relationships turn eventually into nightmares. The struggle between his tolerant and gently ironic approach to life and her strategy of suspicion and attack becomes a kind of war about love and creation which neither can afford to lose. In other words, this is quite an offbeat, wonderful love story. We would like to point out that the play also contains a wealth of excellent *monologue* and *scene material*. (#21060)

(Royalty, $50-$35.)

GOD'S SPIES
(COMEDY)

By DON NIGRO

1 man, 2 women—Interior

This is a truly hilarious send-up of "Christian" television programming by a talented new playwright of wit and imagination. We are "on the air" with one of those talk shows where people are interviewed about their religious conversions, offering testimonials of their faith up to God and the Moral Majority. The first person interview by stalwart Dale Clabby is Calvin Stringer, who discourses on devil worship in popular music. Next comes young Wendy Trumpy, who claims to have talked to God in a belfry. Her testimonial, though, is hardly what Dale expected... Published with *Crossing the Bar*. (#9643)

(Royalty, $15.)

CROSSING THE BAR
(COMEDY)

By DON NIGRO

1 man, 2 women—Interior

Two women sit in a funeral parlor with the corpse of a recently-deceased loved one, saying things like "Doesn't he look like himself", when the corpse sits up, asking for someone named Betty. Who is this Betty, they wonder? God certainly works in mysterious ways... Published with *God's Spies*. (#5935)

(Royalty, $15.)

Other Publications for Your Interest

ADVICE TO THE PLAYERS
(DRAMA)

By BRUCE BONAFEDE

5 men, 1 woman (interracial)—Interior

Seldom has a one-act play created such a sensation as did *Advice to the Players* at Actors Theatre of Louisville's famed Humana Festival of New American Plays. Mr. Bonafede has crafted an ingenious play about two Black South African actors, here in America to perform their internationally-acclaimed production of *Waiting for Godot*. The victims of persecution in their own country, here in the U.S. they become the victims of a different kind of persecution. The anti-apartheid movement wants a strong political gesture—they want the performance cancelled. And, they are willing to go to any lengths to achieve this aim—including threatening the families of the actors back home. Cleverly, Mr. Bonafede juxtaposes the predicament of Didi and Gogo in *Waiting for Godot* with the predicament of the two actors. Both, in an odd, ironic way, are Theatre of the Absurd. "A short play blazing with emotional force and moral complexities . . . taut, searing inquiry into the inequities frequently perpetrated in the name of political justice . . . a stunning moment of theatrical truth."—Louisville Courier-Journal. (#3027)

(Royalty, $25-$20.)

APPROACHING LAVENDAR
(COMIC DRAMA)

By JULIE BECKETT CRUTCHER

3 women—Interior

While their father is marrying his fourth wife sardonic, controlled Jenny and her slightly neurotic housewife-sister Abigail wait in a church vestibule. There they encounter Wren, the spacey ingenue who is about to become their step-sister. The mood of polite tolerance degenerates with comic results as inherent tensions mount and the womens' conflicted feelings about their parents' remarriage surface. The contingent self-discovery results in new understanding and forgiveness, and ultimately reveals the significance of sisterhood. Highly-praised in its debut at the famed Actors Theatre of Louisville, the play was singled out by the Louisville press for its "precise and disquieting vision" as well as its sharp humor, as it "held a capacity audience rapt." (#3649)

(Royalty, $15-$10.)

A TANTALIZING
(DRAMA)

By WILLIAM MASTROSIMONE

1 man, 1 woman—Interior

Originally produced by the amazing Actors Theatre of Louisville, this is a new one-act drama by the author of *The Woolgatherer* and *Extremities*. *A Tantalizing* is about the attempts by a young woman to "save" a street bum, a tattered and crazy old man whom she has dragged in off the street. Like Rose in *Extremities* she, too, has secrets in her closet. What these secrets are is the intriguing mystery in the plot of the play, as we gradually realize why the woman has taken such an interest in the bum. (#22021)

(Royalty, $15-$15.)